COLLECTIBLE DIETZ LANTERNS

by Neil S. Wood

The contents herein were copyrighted 1917 by the R.E. Dietz Company and originally appeared in the "DIETZ LANTERNS CATALOG No. 49 - DEALERS' EDITION"

We wish to thank the R.E. Dietz Company for being a leader in the past creating lanterns which are collectible today

The values listed in this book should only be used as a guide. The prices may vary from one region to another. All prices are also affected by the condition as well as the demand of any given lantern. The publisher does not assume responsibility for any gains or losses that might be incurred as a result of consulting this guide.

ISBN: 0-89538-089-7

Published by: L-W Book Sales
P.O. Box 69
Gas City, IN 46933

Please write for our free catalog of over 700 reference books on antiques and collectibles

1

**ORIGINAL
NO. 0 TUBULAR
LANTERN
(1868)**

... INDEX ...

TO

LANTERN CATALOG

SPECIAL NOTICE

Genuine Dietz Lanterns are Patented and Trade-Marked. They have the Trade Mark

REGISTERED

U. S. PAT. OFF.

stamped in a prominent place. All imitations and infringements will be prosecuted.

R. E. DIETZ COMPANY

FOUNDED 1840

LARGEST MAKERS OF LANTERNS
IN THE WORLD

OFFICERS

JOHN E. DIETZ
PRESIDENT AND GENERAL MANAGER

ROBERT E. DIETZ
VICE-PRESIDENT

FRED W. VAN DUYN
SECRETARY

EDGAR D. PRICE
TREASURER

FRED H. TWOMBLY
ASS'T SECRETARY AND EXPORT MANAGER

FACTORIES

NEW YORK CITY AND SYRACUSE, NEW YORK

MAIN OFFICE

SIXTY LAIGHT STREET, NEW YORK CITY

EXCLUSIVE SALES MANAGER
FOR THE UNITED STATES
WARREN McARTHUR
168 N. MICHIGAN AVENUE, CHICAGO, ILL.

"LITTLE STAR" LANTERN

REG. U. S. PAT. OFFICE—PATENTED

(HOT BLAST)

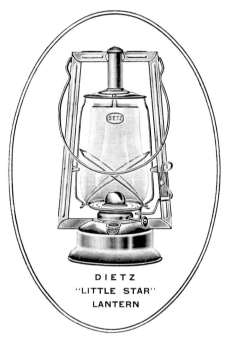

DIETZ
"LITTLE STAR"
LANTERN

NO. 411 BURNER
WING-LOCK CONE, 5/8" WICK

"LITTLE STAR U. S."
GLOBE

FOR KEROSENE

DOZ.

Little Star Lanterns, Bright Tin . . . .

R. E. DIETZ COMPANY - - - - - NEW YORK, U. S. A.

"LITTLE STAR" LANTERN

REG. U. S. PAT. OFFICE—PATENTED

(HOT BLAST)

DIETZ "LITTLE STAR" Lantern is an attractive Square Tube, Hot Blast Lantern, small in size.

It fills a demand for a small Lantern suitable for camping, etc., and is excellent for political campaigns, or night decoration. It is a fine Boy's Lantern and makes a good gift.

The "Little Star" is stocked more and more by Retail Dealers, especially for the Vacation and Christmas trade.

Special features: DIETZ security standing bail, patent brass eyelets, patent safety (wing-lock) burner, patent positive-locking globe lift, large oil-filler and double-seamed solderless dome-shaped oil fount

---

SPECIFICATIONS

Height Over All	11 Inches
Volume of Light by Test	3 C. Power
Size of Wick	⅝ Inch
Oil Used	150° Kerosene
Fount Capacity—Hours	12 Hours
Name of Globe (White, Ruby, Blue and Green)	Dietz "Little Star U.S."
Patented Tinned Steel Burner (Wing-lock Cone)	No. 411
Quantity Packed in One Case	One Dozen

PRICES, WEIGHTS AND MEASUREMENTS ARE GIVEN IN A SEPARATE PRICE LIST

R. E. DIETZ COMPANY - - - - - NEW YORK, U. S. A.

"HY-LO" LANTERN

WITH SIMPLE LIFT
REG. U. S. PAT. OFFICE—PATENTED

(HOT BLAST)

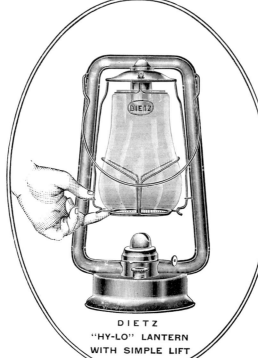

DIETZ
"HY-LO" LANTERN
WITH SIMPLE LIFT

NO. 421 BURNER
HINGED CONE, 5/8" WICK

"FITZALL"
GLOBE

FOR KEROSENE

Hy-Lo Lanterns, Bright Tin . . . . *DOZ.*

R. E. DIETZ COMPANY - - - - - **NEW YORK, U. S. A.**

8

DIETZ
"HY-LO" LANTERN
WITH SIMPLE LIFT
REG. U. S. PAT. OFFICE—PATENTED

(HOT BLAST)

DIETZ "HY-LO" Lantern with its simple globe lift, has an extensive and warranted popularity. No other low-priced make of Lantern compares with it in quality of materials, construction or light-giving ability.

Contractors of public works, railroad and trolley builders, sewer and dam builders and other large users of Lanterns are endorsers of the "Hy-lo."

As an Export Lantern the "Hy-lo" has a very large sale.

Special features: DIETZ patent hinged-cone burner, simple globe lift, large oil-filler, and double-seamed solderless oil fount.

SPECIFICATIONS

Height Over All	13½ Inches
Volume of Light by Test	4 C. Power
Size of Wick	⅝ Inch
Oil Used	150° Kerosene
Fount Capacity—Hours	18 Hours
Name of Globe (White, Ruby, Blue and Green)	Dietz "Fitzall"
Patented Tinned Steel Burner (Hinged Cone)	No. 421
Quantity Packed in One Case	One Dozen

PRICES, WEIGHTS AND MEASUREMENTS ARE GIVEN IN A SEPARATE PRICE LIST

R. E. DIETZ COMPANY   -   -   -   -   -   NEW YORK, U. S. A.

"VICTOR" LANTERN

REG. U. S. PAT. OFFICE—PATENTED

(HOT BLAST)

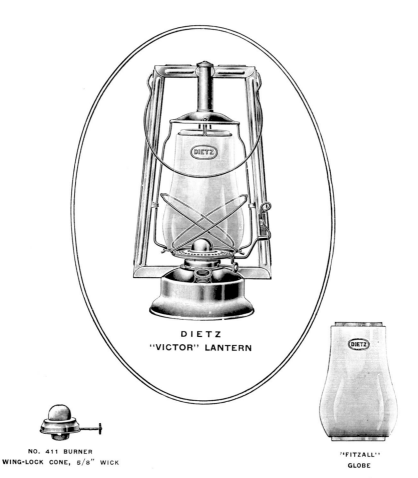

DIETZ
"VICTOR" LANTERN

NO. 411 BURNER
WING-LOCK CONE, 5/8" WICK

"FITZALL"
GLOBE

FOR KEROSENE

	DOZ.
Victor Lanterns, Bright Tin	

R. E. DIETZ COMPANY - - - - - NEW YORK, U. S A.

"VICTOR" LANTERN

REG. U. S. PAT. OFFICE—PATENTED

(HOT BLAST)

SALES OF DIETZ "VICTOR" Square Tube Lanterns, yearly, are greater than all other makes of Hot Blast Lanterns combined.

These Lanterns have lately been improved by the addition of a vertical bead to the tubes, making a much stronger frame.

"Victor" Lanterns burn under the most trying weather conditions.

Special features: DIETZ security standing bail, patent brass eyelets, patent safety (wing-lock) burner, patent positive-locking globe lift, large oil-filler and double-seamed solderless dome-shaped oil fount.

SPECIFICATIONS

Height Over All	$13\frac{1}{4}$ Inches
Volume of Light by Test	4 C. Power
Size of Wick	$\frac{5}{8}$ Inch
Oil Used	150° Kerosene
Fount Capacity—Hours	19 Hours
Name of Globe (White, Ruby, Blue and Green)	Dietz"Fitzall"
Patented Tinned Steel Burner (Wing-lock Cone)	No. 411
Quantity Packed in One Case	One Dozen

PRICES, WEIGHTS AND MEASUREMENTS ARE GIVEN IN A SEPARATE PRICE LIST

R. E. DIETZ COMPANY - - - - - NEW YORK, U. S. A.

"MONARCH" LANTERN

REG. U. S. PAT. OFFICE—PATENTED

(HOT BLAST)

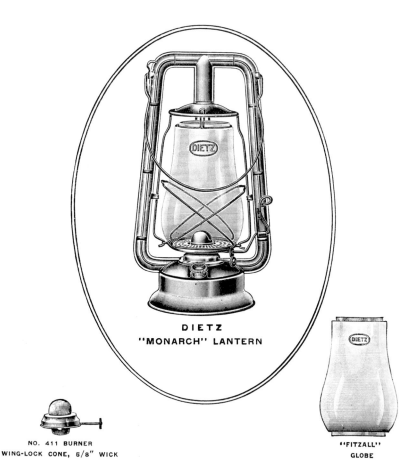

DIETZ
"MONARCH" LANTERN

NO. 411 BURNER
WING-LOCK CONE, 5/8" WICK

"FITZALL"
GLOBE

FOR KEROSENE

DOZ.

Monarch Lanterns, Bright Tin .   .   .   .

R. E. DIETZ COMPANY   -   -   -   -   -   NEW YORK, U. S. A.

"MONARCH" LANTERN

REG. U. S. PAT. OFFICE—PATENTED

(HOT BLAST)

DIETZ "MONARCH" Lantern with round tubes represents the highest development in Hot Blast Lanterns.

Attention is called to the strength of the reinforced air tubes through the use of patented horizontal and vertical beads.

The "Monarch" Lantern is handsomely modeled, has all the latest Lantern improvements and is a Dealer's favorite.

Special features: DIETZ security standing bail, patent brass eyelets, patent safety (wing-lock) burner, patent reinforced tubes, patent positive-locking globe lift, large oil-filler and double-seamed solderless dome-shaped oil fount.

SPECIFICATIONS

Height Over All	13½ Inches
Volume of Light by Test	4 C. Power
Size of Wick	⅝ Inch
Oil Used	150° Kerosene
Fount Capacity—Hours	18 Hours
Name of Globe (White, Ruby, Blue and Green)	Dietz "Fitzall"
Patented Tinned Steel Burner (Wing-lock Cone)	No. 411
Quantity Packed in One Case	One Dozen

PRICES, WEIGHTS AND MEASUREMENTS ARE GIVEN IN A SEPARATE PRICE LIST

R. E. DIETZ COMPANY   -   -   -   -   -   NEW YORK, U. S. A.

"O. K." LANTERN

REG. U. S. PAT. OFFICE—PATENTED

(HOT BLAST)

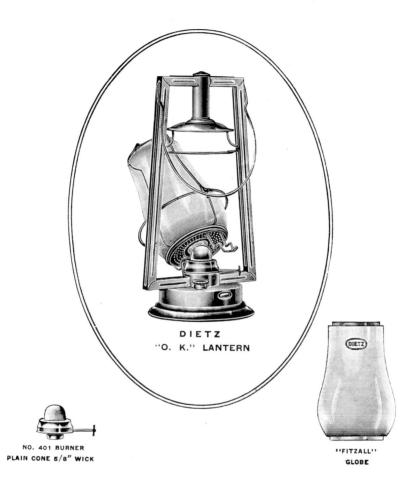

DIETZ
"O. K." LANTERN

NO. 401 BURNER
PLAIN CONE 5/8" WICK

"FITZALL"
GLOBE

FOR KEROSENE

O. K. Lanterns, Bright Tin . . . . *DOZ.*

R. E. DIETZ COMPANY - - - - - NEW YORK, U. S. A.

"O. K." LANTERN

REG. U. S. PAT. OFFICE—PATENTED

(HOT BLAST)

DIETZ "O. K." Lantern has been successfully on the market over 20 years. It is largely used by Contractors.

The "Tip-out" Globe feature in place of a side lift commends the "O. K." to some users who have to clean, trim and light a large number of Lanterns.

Every Lantern Dealer should carry "O. K." Lanterns regularly in stock.

Special features: DIETZ security standing bail, patent brass eyelets, patent plain cone burner, large oil-filler and double-seamed solderless oil fount.

SPECIFICATIONS

Height Over All	13 Inches
Volume of Light by Test	4 C. Power
Size of Wick	⅝ Inch
Oil Used	150° Kerosene
Fount Capacity—Hours	19 Hours
Name of Globe (White, Ruby, Blue or Green) . .	Dietz "Fitzall"
Patented Tinned Steel Burner (Plain Cone) . .	No. 401
Quantity Packed in One Case	One Dozen

PRICES, WEIGHTS AND MEASUREMENTS ARE GIVEN IN A SEPARATE PRICE LIST

R. E. DIETZ COMPANY - - - - - NEW YORK, U. S. A.

"CRYSTAL" LANTERN

WITH GLASS OIL FOUNT

REG. U. S. PAT. OFFICE—PATENTED

(HOT BLAST)

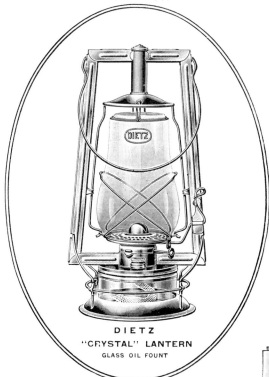

DIETZ
"CRYSTAL" LANTERN

GLASS OIL FOUNT

NO. 421 BURNER
HINGED CONE, 5/8" WICK

GLASS
OIL FOUNT

"FITZALL"
GLOBE

FOR KEROSENE

DOZ.

Crystal Lanterns, Bright Tin . . . . . .

R. E. DIETZ COMPANY - - - - - **NEW YORK, U. S. A.**

"CRYSTAL" LANTERN

WITH GLASS OIL FOUNT
REG. U. S. PAT. OFFICE—PATENTED

(HOT BLAST)

DIETZ "CRYSTAL" Lantern has a Glass Oil Fount which shows the amount of oil on hand. It is the only Glass Fount Lantern on the market.

The Fount is detachable and can be quickly replaced if broken.

The "Crystal" is a good all-around Lantern and a ready seller. Dealers find a good "Talking Point" in the glass oil container.

Special features: DIETZ security standing bail, patent brass eyelets, patent hinged-cone burner, patent positive-locking globe lift, large oil-filler and glass oil fount with wire guard.

SPECIFICATIONS

Height Over All	14 Inches
Volume of Light by Test	4 C. Power
Size of Wick	5/8 Inch
Oil Used	150° Kerosene
Fount Capacity—Hours	15 Hours
Name of Globe (White, Ruby, Blue and Green) . .	Dietz"Fitzall"
Patented Tinned Steel Burner (Hinged Cone) . .	No. 421
Quantity Packed in One Case	One Dozen

PRICES, WEIGHTS AND MEASUREMENTS ARE GIVEN IN A SEPARATE PRICE LIST

R. E. DIETZ COMPANY   -   -   -   -   -   NEW YORK, U. S. A.

"IRON CLAD" LANTERN

WITH HEAVY IRON BASE

REG. U. S. PAT. OFFICE—PATENTED

(HOT BLAST)

DIETZ
"IRON CLAD" LANTERN
HEAVY IRON BASE

NO. 421 BURNER
HINGED CONE, 5/8" WICK

IRON BASE

"FITZALL"
GLOBE

FOR KEROSENE

DOZ.

Iron Clad Lanterns, Bright Tin . . . . . .

R. E. DIETZ COMPANY - - - - - NEW YORK, U. S. A.

"IRON CLAD" LANTERN
WITH HEAVY IRON BASE
REG. U. S. PAT. OFFICE—PATENTED

(HOT BLAST)

D IETZ "I R O N C L A D" Lantern is an ideal Contractor's Lantern for rough usage.

A heavy Iron Base attached to the tubes by braces gives the Lantern strength and prevents its being blown over.

In the building of the Panama Canal, Dietz "Iron Clad" Lanterns were used exclusively, many thousands being purchased by the U. S. Government.

Special features: DIETZ security standing bail, patent brass eyelets, patent hinged-cone burner, patent positive-locking globe lift, large oil-filler, braced frame and heavy japanned iron base.

SPECIFICATIONS

Height Over All	13¼ Inches
Volume of Light by Test	4 C. Power
Size of Wick	⅝ Inch
Oil Used	150° Kerosene
Fount Capacity—Hours	16 Hours
Name of Globe (White, Ruby, Blue and Green) . .	Dietz "Fitzall"
Patented Tinned Steel Burner (Hinged Cone) .	No. 421
Quantity Packed in One Case	One Dozen

PRICES, WEIGHTS AND MEASUREMENTS ARE GIVEN IN A SEPARATE PRICE LIST

R. E. DIETZ COMPANY - - - - - **NEW YORK, U. S. A.**

NO. 2 "ROYAL" LANTERN
ONE INCH WICK—5 CANDLE POWER
REG. U. S. PAT. OFFICE—PATENTED

(HOT BLAST)

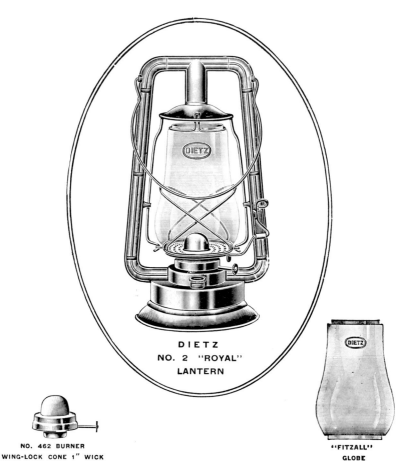

DIETZ
NO. 2 "ROYAL"
LANTERN

NO. 462 BURNER
WING-LOCK CONE 1" WICK

"FITZALL"
GLOBE

FOR KEROSENE

DOZ.

No. 2 Royal Lanterns, Bright Tin .   .   .   .   .   .

R. E. DIETZ COMPANY   -   -   -   -   -   -   NEW YORK, U. S. A.

NO. 2 "ROYAL" LANTERN

ONE INCH WICK—5 CANDLE POWER

REG. U. S. PAT. OFFICE—PATENTED

(HOT BLAST)

DIETZ No. 2 "ROYAL" Lantern is a larger size of the "Monarch" type. It takes a one-inch wick.

The No. 2 "Royal" gives a light of five candle power, the largest light of any Hot-Blast Lantern.

As a Dealer's proposition, the No. 2 "Royal" sells well. It fills a demand for a large Lantern costing less than a Cold Blast Lantern.

Special features: DIETZ security standing bail, patent brass eyelets, patent wing-lock burner, patent reinforced tubes, patent positive-locking globe lift, large oil-filler and double-seamed solderless oil fount.

SPECIFICATIONS

Height Over All	13½ Inches
Volume of Light by Test	5 C. Power
Size of Wick	1 Inch
Oil Used	150° Kerosene
Fount Capacity—Hours	20 Hours
Name of Globe (White, Ruby, Blue and Green)	Dietz "Fitzall"
Patented Tinned Steel Burner (Wing-lock Cone)	No. 462
Quantity Packed in One Case	One Dozen

PRICES, WEIGHTS AND MEASUREMENTS ARE GIVEN IN A SEPARATE PRICE LIST

R E. DIETZ COMPANY   -   -   -   -   -   NEW YORK, U. S. A.

"BESTOV" HAND LAMP

REG. U. S. PAT. OFFICE—PATENTED

(COLD BLAST)

DIETZ
BESTOV" HAND LAMP
PORTABLE

NO. 101 CHIMNEY BURNER
5/8" WICK

NO. 1 LIP
CHIMNEY

FOR KEROSENE

DOZ.

Bestov Hand Lamps, Bright Tin . . . .

R. E. DIETZ COMPANY - - - - - NEW YORK, U. S. A.

"BESTOV" HAND LAMP

REG. U. S. PAT. OFFICE—PATENTED

(COLD BLAST)

DIETZ "BESTOV" Hand Lamp is a fine light giver. As a Portable it is not affected by draughts, owing to the balanced air supply taken through the side tube.

The "Bestov" makes a good Table Lamp, having a table base, and may be used as a Wall Lamp. It is all metal except the chimney. With a little care it will last for years.

Dealers find the "Bestov" a ready seller as a novelty, and the sale of a single Lamp makes many more.

Special features: DIETZ patent reinforced air tube, large oil-filler and double-seamed solderless dome-shaped oil fount with table base.

SPECIFICATIONS

Height Over All	10 Inches
Volume of Light by Test	6 C. Power
Size of Wick	⅝ Inch
Oil Used	150° Kerosene
Name of Chimney	No. 1 Lip
Dietz Tinned Steel Burner	No. 101
Quantity Packed in One Case, Complete with Chimneys	One Dozen

PRICES, WEIGHTS AND MEASUREMENTS ARE GIVEN IN A SEPARATE PRICE LIST

R. E. DIETZ COMPANY - - - - - **NEW YORK, U. S. A.**

TRAFFIC SIGNAL LANTERNS
YOU SEE THEM EVERYWHERE

R. E. DIETZ COMPANY - - - - - NEW YORK, U. S. A.

TRAFFIC SIGNAL LANTERNS
YOU SEE THEM EVERYWHERE

FOR TRAFFIC SIGNS of the "Go-Stop" variety the Dietz "Traffic Signal" Lantern with two ruby and two green lenses is unexcelled.

GANGWAY AND INTERSECTING corner signs do not require a special pattern light, a good lantern with a green globe fulfilling all needs.

DIETZ "VESTA," "Iron Clad," "Little Wizard," "Junior," and "Little Star" Lanterns, with green globes are largely used as traffic signals; any Dietz Lantern with a green globe may be used.

DIETZ Lanterns give a clear light, they do not smoke or blow out.

R. E. DIETZ COMPANY   -   -   -   -   -   NEW YORK, U. S. A.

"JUNIOR" LANTERN

REG. U. S. PAT. OFFICE—PATENTED

(COLD BLAST)

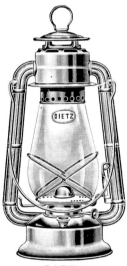

**DIETZ
"JUNIOR" LANTERN**

**DIETZ
"JUNIOR" LANTERN
WITH GLOBE RAISED
(BRASS)**

NO. 201 BURNER
WING-LOCK CONE, 5/8" WICK

"JUNIOR"
GLOBE

FOR KEROSENE

DOZ.

Junior Lanterns, Bright Tin . . . .

Junior Lanterns, Brass . . . . . .

Junior Lanterns, Nickel-plated on Brass . . . . .

R. E. DIETZ COMPANY - - - - - **NEW YORK, U. S. A.**

"JUNIOR" LANTERN

REG. U. S. PAT. OFFICE—PATENTED

(COLD BLAST)

DIETZ "JUNIOR" is a small "Cold Blast" Lantern and gives a remarkable light for its size—six candle power.

In spite of numerous imitations, more Dietz "Junior" Lanterns are sold than of all similar Lanterns combined.

The popularity of the "Junior" is world-wide. The brass and nickel-plated styles are practically indestructible, and with care will last a life-time.

Special features: DIETZ security standing bail, patent brass eyelets, patent safety (wing-lock) burner, patent reinforced tubes, patent globe lift on inside of frame, large oil-filler and double-seamed dome-shaped solderless oil fount.

SPECIFICATIONS

Height Over All	12 Inches
Volume of Light by Test	6 C. Power
Size of Wick	5⁄8 Inch
Oil Used	150° Kerosene
Fount Capacity—Hours	13 Hours
Name of Globe (White, Ruby, Blue and Green) . .	Dietz "Junior"
Patented Tinned Steel Burner (Wing-lock Cone) .	No. 201
Quantity Packed in One Case	One Dozen

PRICES, WEIGHTS AND MEASUREMENTS ARE GIVEN IN A SEPARATE PRICE LIST

R. E. DIETZ COMPANY - - - - - - **NEW YORK, U. S. A.**

NO. 2 "CRESCENT" LANTERN

REG. U. S. PAT. OFFICE—PATENTED

(COLD BLAST)

DIETZ
NO. 2 "CRESCENT"
LANTERN

NO. 262 BURNER
WING-LOCK CONE 1" WICK

"FITZALL"
GLOBE

FOR KEROSENE

No. 2 Crescent Lanterns, Bright Tin . . . . .

DOZ.

R. E. DIETZ COMPANY -   -   -   -   -   NEW YORK, U. S. A.

NO. 2 "CRESCENT" LANTERN

REG. U. S. PAT. OFFICE—PATENTED

(COLD BLAST)

THE DEMAND for a low-priced Lantern of the "Cold Blast" type, is satisfied with the Dietz No. 2 "Crescent."

The No. 2 "Crescent" Lantern is well constructed and a good light-giver. It is superior to the many imitations of Dietz Cold Blast Lanterns on the market, and costs less money.

Contractors and other buyers of Lanterns in quantity needing a large Lantern at a low price, buy the No. 2 "Crescent."

Special features: DIETZ security standing bail, patent brass eyelets, patent safety (wing-lock) burner, patent globe lift on inside of frame, large oil-filler and double-seamed solderless oil fount.

SPECIFICATIONS

Height Over All	15 Inches
Volume of Light by Test	10 C. Power
Size of Wick	1 Inch
Oil Used	150° Kerosene
Fount Capacity—Hours	18 Hours
Name of Globe (White, Ruby, Blue and Green)	Dietz "Fitzall"
Patented Tinned Steel Burner (Wing-lock Cone)	No. 262
Quantity Packed in One Case	Half Dozen

PRICES, WEIGHTS AND MEASUREMENTS ARE GIVEN IN A SEPARATE PRICE LIST

R. E. DIETZ COMPANY   -   -   -   -   -   NEW YORK, U. S. A.

NO. 2 "BLIZZARD" LANTERN

ONE INCH WICK—10 CANDLE POWER

REG. U. S. PAT. OFFICE—PATENTED

(COLD BLAST)

DIETZ
NO. 2 "BLIZZARD"
LANTERN

NO. 272 WING-LOCK BURNER
RISING CONE, 1" WICK

"BLIZZARD"
LOC-NOB GLOBE

DIETZ
NO. 2 "BLIZZARD"
WITH GLOBE RAISED
(BRASS FOUNT AND TOP)

FOR KEROSENE

DOZ.

No. 2 Blizzard Lanterns, Bright Tin . . . . .

No. 2 Blizzard Lanterns, Brass Fount and Top . . . .

R. E. DIETZ COMPANY - - - - - NEW YORK, U. S. A.

NO. 2 "BLIZZARD" LANTERN

ONE INCH WICK—10 CANDLE POWER
REG. U. S. PAT. OFFICE—PATENTED

(COLD BLAST)

DIETZ FAMOUS No. 2 "BLIZZARD" Lantern first appeared on the market in 1898 and has been continually improved.

Two attractive new features are the Wing-lock Rising Cone Burner, exposing the wick for trimming and lighting, and the Patent "Loc-Nob" Globe.

The No. 2 "Blizzard" gives a clear white light of ten candle power. While other styles are popular, the "Blizzard" remains a big favorite with Lantern Dealers.

Special features: DIETZ security standing bail, patent brass eyelets, patent safety (wing-lock) rising cone burner, patent reinforced tubes, patent globe lift on inside of frame, large oil-filler, patent locking globe and double-seamed solderless dome-shaped oil fount.

SPECIFICATIONS

Height Over All	14¾ Inches
Volume of Light by Test	10 C. Power
Size of Wick	1 Inch
Oil Used	150° Kerosene
Fount Capacity—Hours	20 Hours
Name of Globe (White, Ruby, Blue and Green)	Dietz "Blizzard" (Loc-Nob
Patented Tinned Steel Burner (Rising Cone)	No. 272
Quantity Packed in One Case . . .	Half Dozen

PRICES, WEIGHTS AND MEASUREMENTS ARE GIVEN IN A SEPARATE PRICE LIST

R. E. DIETZ COMPANY   -   -   -   -   -   NEW YORK, U. S. A.

NO. 2 LARGE FOUNT "BLIZZARD"

BURNS 40 HOURS

REG. U. S. PAT. OFFICE—PATENTED

(COLD BLAST)

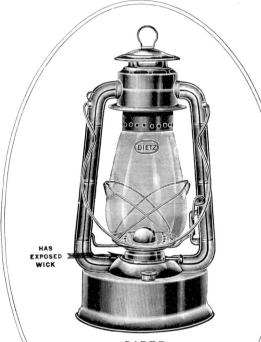

HAS
EXPOSED
WICK

DIETZ
NO. 2 LARGE FOUNT "BLIZZARD"
LANTERN

"BLIZZARD"
LOC-NOB GLOBE

NO. 272 WING-LOCK BURNER
RISING CONE, 1" WICK

FOR KEROSENE

DOZ.

Special No. 2 Blizzard Lanterns, Bright Tin . . . .

R. E. DIETZ COMPANY - - - - - NEW YORK, U. S. A.

NO. 2 LARGE FOUNT "BLIZZARD"

BURNS 40 HOURS
REG. U. S. PAT. OFFICE—PATENTED

(COLD BLAST)

DIETZ NO. 2 Large Fount "Blizzard" Lantern burns for almost two days with one filling. It is largely used by fishermen for lighting channel marks, etc.

The No. 2 Large Fount "Blizzard" has two new Dealer's "Talking Points" besides the large fount—a Dietz Wing-lock "Rising Cone" Burner and the Dietz Patent Loc-Nob Globe. The yearly sales show a growing demand for lanterns with a large oil capacity.

Special features: DIETZ security standing bail, patent brass eyelets, patent safety (wing-lock) rising-cone burner, patent reinforced tubes, patent globe lift on inside of frame, large oil-filler, patent locking globe and extra large double-seamed solderless, dome-shaped oil fount.

SPECIFICATIONS

Height Over All	15 Inches
Volume of Light by Test	10 C. Power
Size of Wick	I Inch
Oil Used	150° Kerosene
Fount Capacity—Hours	40 Hours
Name of Globe (White, Ruby, Blue and Green)	Dietz "Blizzard" (Loc-Nob)
Patented Tinned Steel Burner (Rising Cone)	No. 272
Quantity Packed in One Case . . .	Half Dozen

PRICES, WEIGHTS AND MEASUREMENTS ARE GIVEN IN A SEPARATE PRICE LIST

R. E. DIETZ COMPANY   -   -   -   -   -   NEW YORK, U S A.

"LITTLE WIZARD" LANTERN

REG. U. S. PAT. OFFICE—PATENTED

(COLD BLAST)

DIETZ
"LITTLE WIZARD"
LANTERN

NOTE
EXPOSED
WICK

DIETZ
"LITTLE WIZARD"
LANTERN
WITH GLOBE RAISED

NO. 211 WING-LOCK BURNER
RISING CONE, 5/8" WICK

"LITTLE WIZARD"
LOC-NOB GLOBE

FOR KEROSENE

DOZ.

Little Wizard Lanterns, Bright Tin . . . . .

R. E. DIETZ COMPANY - - - - - **NEW YORK, U. S. A.**

"LITTLE WIZARD" LANTERN

REG. U. S. PAT. OFFICE—PATENTED

(COLD BLAST)

DIETZ "LITTLE WIZARD" makes a quick conquest of a buyer looking for a handy all-round small Lantern.

It is under 12 inches in height, has a large oil fount, the wick is exposed for trimming and lighting, and it has the Dietz Loc-Nob short globe in which the hand may be inserted for cleaning.

The "Little Wizard" gives double the light of a Hot Blast Lantern using the same size of wick.

Special features: DIETZ security standing bail, patent brass eyelets, patent safety (wing-lock) rising-cone burner, patent reinforced tubes, patent globe lift on inside of frame, large oil-filler, patent locking globe and double-seamed solderless, dome-shaped oil fount.

SPECIFICATIONS

Height Over All	11½ Inches
Volume of Light by Test . . .	6 C. Power
Size of Wick	⅝ Inch
Oil Used	150° Kerosene
Fount Capacity—Hours . . .	18 Hours
Name of Globe (White, Ruby, Blue and Green) Dietz "Little Wizard" (Loc-Nob)	
Patented Tinned Steel Burner (Rising Cone) No. 211	
Quantity Packed in One Case . .	One Dozen

PRICES, WEIGHTS AND MEASUREMENTS ARE GIVEN IN A SEPARATE PRICE LIST

R. E. DIETZ COMPANY - - - - - NEW YORK, U. S. A.

NO. 2 "WIZARD" LANTERN

REG. U. S. PAT. OFFICE—PATENTED

(COLD BLAST)

**DIETZ
NO. 2 "WIZARD"
LANTERN**

**NO. 2 "WIZARD"
WITH GLOBE RAISED
(BRASS FOUNT AND TOP)**

NO. 272 WING-LOCK BURNER
RISING CONE, 1" WICK

"D-LITE"
LOC-NOB GLOBE

FOR KEROSENE

DOZ.

No. 2 Wizard Lanterns, Bright Tin . . . . .

No. 2 Wizard Lanterns, Brass Fount and Top . . . .

R. E. DIETZ COMPANY - - - - - **NEW YORK, U. S. A.**

NO. 2 "WIZARD" LANTERN

REG. U. S. PAT. OFFICE—PATENTED

(COLD BLAST)

DIETZ No. 2 "WIZARD" Lantern is a splendid example of the best of the Lantern maker's art.

In height it is no greater than a common Hot Blast Lantern, but it gives almost three times the candle-power.

The No. 2 "Wizard" is mechanically perfect. It has the Loc-Nob short Globe and is the easiest of Lanterns to clean, fill and light. A prime favorite with Lantern Dealers.

Special features: DIETZ security standing bail, patent brass eyelets, patent safety (wing-lock) rising cone burner, patent reinforced tubes, patent globe lift on inside of frame, large oil-filler, patent locking short globe and double-seamed solderless dome-shaped oil fount.

SPECIFICATIONS

Height Over All	13¼ Inches
Volume of Light by Test	10 C. Power
Size of Wick	1 Inch
Oil Used	150° Kerosene
Fount Capacity—Hours	20 Hours
Name of Globe (White, Ruby, Blue and Green)	Dietz "D-Lite" (Loc-Nob)
Patented Tinned Steel Burner (Rising Cone)	No. 272
Quantity Packed in One Case . . .	One Dozen

PRICES, WEIGHTS AND MEASUREMENTS ARE GIVEN IN A SEPARATE PRICE LIST

R. E. DIETZ COMPANY - - - - - **NEW YORK, U. S. A.**

NO. 2 LARGE FOUNT "WIZARD"

BURNS 40 HOURS
REG. U. S. PAT. OFFICE—PATENTED

(COLD BLAST)

DIETZ
NO 2 LARGE FOUNT
"WIZARD" LANTERN

NO. 272 WING-LOCK BURNER
RISING CONE 1" WICK

"D-LITE"
LOC-NOB GLOBE

FOR KEROSENE

	DOZ.
No. 2 Large Fount Wizard Lanterns, Bright Tin . . .	
No. 2 Large Fount Wizard, Brass Fount and Top . . .	

R. E. DIETZ COMPANY - - - - - - **NEW YORK, U. S. A.**

NO. 2 LARGE FOUNT "WIZARD"

BURNS 40 HOURS

REG. U. S. PAT. OFFICE—PATENTED

(COLD BLAST)

ATTENTION is called to the new Large Fount Lantern, Dietz No. 2 Large Fount "Wizard.

This Lantern burns 40 hours with one filling and gives a light of ten candle-power.

The No. 2 Large Fount "Wizard" has all the latest Lantern improvements in addition to the large oil container and is an attractive selling proposition.

Special features: DIETZ security standing bail, patent brass eyelets, patent safety (wing-lock) rising cone burner, patent reinforced tubes, patent globe lift on inside of frame, large oil-filler, patent locking short globe and extra large double-seamed solderless dome-shaped oil fount.

SPECIFICATIONS

Height Over All . . . . . . 13¾ Inches

Volume of Light by Test . . . . . 10 Candle Power

Size of Wick . . . . 1 Inch

Oil Used . . . . 150° Kerosene

Fount Capacity—Hours . . . . . 40 Hours

Name of Globe (White, Ruby, Blue and Green) . Dietz D-Lite (Loc-nob)

Patented Tinned Steel Burner . . . . No. 272

Quantity Packed in One Case . . . . Half Dozen

PRICES, WEIGHTS AND MEASUREMENTS ARE GIVEN IN A SEPARATE PRICE LIST

R. E. DIETZ COMPANY - - - - - NEW YORK, U. S. A.

NO. 2 "D-LITE" LANTERN

REG. U. S. PAT. OFFICE—PATENTED

(COLD BLAST)

DIETZ
NO. 2 "D-LITE"
LANTERN

NOTE
EXPOSED
WICK

NO. 2 "D-LITE"
BRASS FOUNT AND DOME

NO. 282 BURNER
RISING CONE, 1" WICK

"D-LITE"
LOC-NOB GLOBE

FOR KEROSENE

DOZ.

No. 2 D-Lite Lanterns, Bright Tin .   .   .   .   .

No. 2 D-Lite Lanterns, Brass Fount and Dome .   .   .

R. E. DIETZ COMPANY - - - - - **NEW YORK, U. S. A.**

NO. 2 "D-LITE" LANTERN

REG. U. S. PAT. OFFICE—PATENTED

(COLD BLAST)

DIETZ No. 2 "D-LITE" Lantern with top lift and telescoping canopy is unique among Lanterns.

The appearance of this Lantern in 1913 with its short bowl-shaped Globe and exposed wick marked a new departure in the Lantern art.

The No. 2 "D-lite" is the highest priced Cold Blast Lantern marketed, and has an increasing sale among the class of buyers who demand the best regardless of price.

Special features: DIETZ security standing bail, patent brass eyelets, patent safety rising coneburner, patent reinforced tubes, patent top lift; globe and rising cone tip out; large oil-filler, patent locking short globe and double-seamed, solderless, dome-shaped oil fount.

SPECIFICATIONS

Height Over All	13¼ Inches
Volume of Light by Test	10 C. Power
Size of Wick	1 Inch
Oil Used	150° Kerosene
Fount Capacity—Hours	20 Hours
Name of Globe (White, Ruby, Blue and Green)	Dietz "D-Lite" (Loc-Nob)
Patented Tinned Steel Burner (Rising Cone)	No. 282
Quantity Packed in One Case . . .	Half Dozen

PRICES, WEIGHTS AND MEASUREMENTS ARE GIVEN IN A SEPARATE PRICE LIST

R. E. DIETZ COMPANY - - - - - **NEW YORK, U. S. A.**

"BUCKEYE" DASH LANTERN

REG. U. S. PAT. OFFICE—PATENTED

(HOT BLAST)

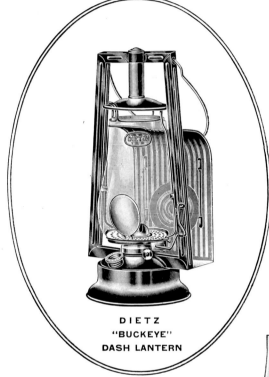

DIETZ
"BUCKEYE"
DASH LANTERN

NO 411 BURNER
WING-LOCK CONE, 5/8" WICK

MAGNIFYING LENS
ON PLATE

"FITZALL"
GLOBE

FOR KEROSENE

DOZ.

Buckeye Dash Lanterns, Black Enamel .   .   .   .   .   .

R. E. DIETZ COMPANY   -   -   -   -   -   NEW YORK, U. S A.

"BUCKEYE" DASH LANTERN

REG. U. S. PAT. OFFICE—PATENTED

(HOT BLAST)

DIETZ "BUCKEYE" Dash Lantern has been popular for several decades with those drivers whose business takes them abroad at night.

The "Buckeye" is low-priced but strongly made and a good light-giver. It fastens to the Dash by a spring clip on the back of the bright tin reflector.

It may also be hung on the wall as a Wall Lantern or carried about by the bail as a Hand Lantern. Nicely finished in Black Enamel.

Special features: DIETZ security standing bail, patent brass eyelets, patent safety (wing-lock) burner, patent positive-locking globe lift, magnifying bullseye lens, large oil-filler and double-seamed solderless dome-shaped oil fount with safety oil well.

SPECIFICATIONS

Height Over All	13¼ Inches
Reflected Light by Test	10 C. Power
Size of Wick	⅝ Inch
Oil Used	150° Kerosene
Fount Capacity—Hours	19 Hours
Name of Globe	Dietz "Fitzall"
Patented Tinned Steel Burner (Wing-lock Cone)	No. 411
Size of Magnifying Bullseye Lens	2¼ Inches
Quantity Packed in One Case	Half Dozen

PRICES, WEIGHTS AND MEASUREMENTS ARE GIVEN IN A SEPARATE PRICE LIST

R. E. DIETZ COMPANY   -   -   -   -   -   NEW YORK, U. S. A.

NO. 2 "BLIZZARD" DASH LANTERN

REG. U. S. PAT. OFFICE—PATENTED

(COLD BLAST)

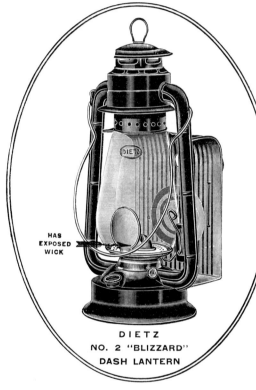

DIETZ
NO. 2 "BLIZZARD"
DASH LANTERN

NO. 272 WING-LOCK BURNER
RISING CONE, 1" WICK

MAGNIFYING LENS
ON PLATE

"BLIZZARD"
GLOBE

FOR KEROSENE

DOZ.

No. 2 Blizzard Dash Lanterns, Black Enamel . . . .

R. E. DIETZ COMPANY - - - - - - **NEW YORK, U. S. A.**

NO. 2 "BLIZZARD" DASH LANTERN

REG. U. S. PAT. OFFICE—PATENTED

(COLD BLAST)

DIETZ No. 2 "BLIZZARD" Dash Lantern sells well with the class of night-drivers who like a big Lantern and a big light.

It is a Dash Lantern and Hand Lantern in combination, having a bail in addition to the dash spring clip on the back of the bright tin reflector.

Also, as a Wall Lantern, it may be hung up on a nail in a room or on a tent post. Nicely finished in Black Enamel.

Special features: DIETZ security standing bail, patent brass eyelets, patent safety (wing-lock) rising cone burner, patent reinforced tubes, patent globe lift on inside of frame, magnifying bullseye lens, large oil-filler and double-seamed solderless dome-shaped oil fount with safety oil well.

SPECIFICATIONS

Height Over All	14¾ Inches
Reflected Light by Test	20 C. Power
Size of Wick	1 Inch
Oil Used	150° Kerosene
Fount Capacity—Hours	18 Hours
Name of Globe	Dietz "Blizzard"
Patented Tinned Steel Burner (Rising Cone)	No. 272
Size of Magnifying Bullseye Lens	2¼ Inches
Quantity Packed in One Case	Half Dozen

PRICES, WEIGHTS AND MEASUREMENTS ARE GIVEN IN A SEPARATE PRICE LIST

R. E. DIETZ COMPANY   NEW YORK, U. S. A.

"BEACON" DASH LANTERN

REG. U. S. PAT. OFFICE—PATENTED

(HOT BLAST)

DIETZ
"BEACON"
DASH LANTERN

NO. 651 WING-LOCK BURNER
LONG CONE, 5/8" WICK

6" SILVERED REFLECTOR

"FITZALL"
GLOBE

FOR KEROSENE

DOZ.

Beacon Dash Lanterns, Black Enamel . . . . .

"BEACON" DASH LANTERN

REG. U. S. PAT. OFFICE—PATENTED

(HOT BLAST)

DIETZ "BEACON" Dash Lantern, formerly known as the No. 0 Reflector Lantern, is an old-time favorite with Dealers.

It has a large bright tin hood, containing a five-inch silvered glass reflector, and throws a strong light ahead. In use it fastens to the dash by a spring clip.

The "Beacon" Dash is strongly made and braced. It may also be used as a Hand Lantern or a Wall Lantern.

Special features: DIETZ security standing bail, patent brass eyelets, patent safety long cone (wing-lock) burner, 5-inch silvered glass reflector, large oil-filler and double-seamed solderless oil fount with safety oil well.

SPECIFICATIONS

Height Over All	13¼ Inches
Reflected Light by Test	20 C. Power
Size of Wick	⅝ Inch
Oil Used	150° Kerosene
Fount Capacity—Hours	20 Hours
Name of Globe	Dietz "Fitzall"
Tinned Steel Burner (Long Cone) . . .	No. 551
Silvered Glass Reflector	5 Inches
Quantity Packed in One Case . . .	Half Dozen

PRICES, WEIGHTS AND MEASUREMENTS ARE GIVEN IN A SEPARATE PRICE LIST

R. E. DIETZ COMPANY - - - - - **NEW YORK, U. S. A.**

"VICTOR" WAGON LANTERN

REG. U. S. PAT. OFFICE—PATENTED

(HOT BLAST)

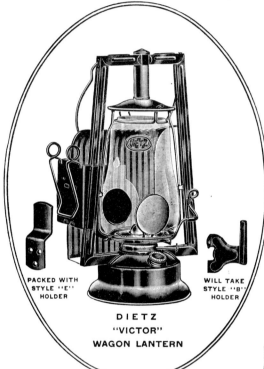

PACKED WITH
STYLE "E"
HOLDER

WILL TAKE
STYLE "B"
HOLDER

**DIETZ
"VICTOR"
WAGON LANTERN**

**NO. 411 BURNER
WING-LOCK CONE, 5/8" WICK**

**MAGNIFYING LENS
ON PLATE**

**"FITZALL"
GLOBE**

FOR KEROSENE

Made left hand only

DOZ.

Victor Wagon Lanterns, Black Enamel . . . . .

R. E. DIETZ COMPANY - - - - - NEW YORK, U. S. A.

"VICTOR" WAGON LANTERN

REG. U. S. PAT. OFFICE—PATENTED

(HOT BLAST)

DIETZ "VICTOR" Wagon Lantern is adaptable to most kinds of commercial vehicles and complies with all night-driving laws.

In use it is located on the left hand side of the wagon or carriage and gives a good light on the road ahead. A 2¼-inch ruby rear lens makes an effective danger signal.

A combination holder permits the use of a round or flat bracket in fastening the Lantern in position on a vehicle. Nicely finished in Black Enamel.

Special features: DIETZ security standing bail, patent brass eyelets, patent safety (wing-lock) burner, patent positive-locking globe lift, magnifying bullseye lens, ruby rear lens, combination holder, large oil-filler and double-seamed solderless dome-shaped oil fount with safety oil well.

SPECIFICATIONS

Height Over All	13¼ Inches
Reflected Light by Test	10 C. Power
Size of Wick	⅝ Inch
Oil Used	150° Kerosene
Fount Capacity—Hours	19 Hours
Name of Globe	Dietz "Fitzall"
Patented Tinned Steel Burner (Wing-lock Cone) .	No. 411
Size of Magnifying Bullseye Lens	2¼ Inches
Size of Ruby Rear Lens	2¼ Inches
Quantity Packed in One Case	Half Dozen

PRICES, WEIGHTS AND MEASUREMENTS ARE GIVEN IN A SEPARATE PRICE LIST

R. E. DIETZ COMPANY - - - - - NEW YORK, U. S. A.

"JUNIOR" WAGON LANTERN

REG. U. S. PAT. OFFICE—PATENTED

(COLD BLAST)

PACKED WITH
STYLE "E"
HOLDER

WILL TAKE
STYLE "B"
HOLDER

DIETZ
"JUNIOR"
WAGON LANTERN

NO. 201 BURNER
WING-LOCK CONE, 5/8" WICK

MAGNIFYING LENS
ON PLATE

"JUNIOR"
GLOBE

FOR KEROSENE

Order for Right or Left Hand as Wanted

Junior Wagon Lanterns, Black Enamel . . . . .   *DOZ.*

R. E. DIETZ COMPANY - - - - - **NEW YORK, U. S. A.**

"JUNIOR" WAGON LANTERN

REG. U. S. PAT. OFFICE—PATENTED

(COLD BLAST)

DIETZ "JUNIOR" Wagon Lantern is but twelve inches high, is attractive in appearance and a seller everywhere.

The "Junior" is made both right and left hand and many sales are made in pairs. It shows a 2¼-inch danger signal to the rear and complies with all night-driving laws.

A combination holder permits the use of a round or flat bracket in fastening the Lantern in position on a vehicle. Nicely finished in Black Enamel.

Special features: DIETZ security standing bail, patent brass eyelets, patent safety (wing-lock) burner, patent reinforced tubes, patent globe lift on inside of frame, magnifying bullseye lens, ruby rear lens, combination holder, large oil-filler and double-seamed solderless dome-shaped oil fount with safety oil well.

SPECIFICATIONS

Height Over All	12 Inches
Reflected Light by Test	10 C. Power
Size of Wick	⅝ Inch
Oil Used	150° Kerosene
Fount Capacity—Hours	13 Hours
Name of Globe	Dietz "Junior"
Patented Tinned Steel Burner (Wing-lock Cone)	No. 201
Size of Ruby Rear Lens	2¼ Inches
Size of Magnifying Bullseye Lens	2¼ Inches
Quantity Packed in One Case	Half Dozen

PRICES, WEIGHTS AND MEASUREMENTS ARE GIVEN IN A SEPARATE PRICE LIST

R. E. DIETZ COMPANY - - - - - **NEW YORK, U. S. A.**

"ROADSTER" WAGON LANTERN

REG. U. S. PAT. OFFICE—PATENTED

(COLD BLAST)

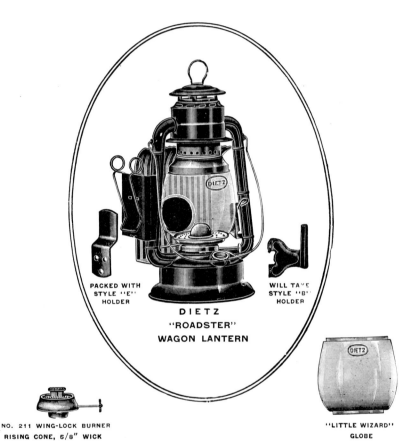

PACKED WITH
STYLE "E"
HOLDER

WILL TAKE
STYLE "B"
HOLDER

D I E T Z
"ROADSTER"
WAGON LANTERN

NO. 211 WING-LOCK BURNER
RISING CONE, 5/8" WICK

"LITTLE WIZARD"
GLOBE

FOR KEROSENE

Made for Left Hand only

DOZ.

Roadster Wagon Lanterns, Black Enamel .   .   .   .   .

R. E. DIETZ COMPANY - - - - - - **NEW YORK, U. S. A.**

"ROADSTER" WAGON LANTERN

REG. U. S. PAT. OFFICE—PATENTED

(COLD BLAST)

Dietz "ROADSTER" Wagon Lantern is new and possesses all the elements of a popular seller. It burns 18 hours with one filling.

The "Roadster" is of the "short globe" type. It is made both right and left hand and complies with all night-driving laws, having a 2¼-inch danger signal to the rear.

A combination holder permits the use of a round or flat bracket in fastening the Lantern in position on a vehicle. Nicely finished in Black Enamel.

Special features: DIETZ security standing bail, patent brass eyelets, patent short globe, patent safety rising cone (wing-lock) burner, patent reinforced tubes, patent globe lift on inside of frame, ruby rear lens, combination holder, large oil-filler and double-seamed solderless dome-shaped oil fount with safety oil well.

SPECIFICATIONS

Height Over All	11½ Inches
Reflected Light by Test	10 C. Power
Size of Wick	⅝ Inch
Oil Used	150° Kerosene
Fount Capacity—Hours	18 Hours
Name of Globe	Dietz "Little Wizard"
Patented Tinned Steel Burner (Rising Cone)	No. 211
Size of Ruby Rear Lens	2¼ Inches
Quantity Packed in One Case	One Dozen

PRICES, WEIGHTS AND MEASUREMENTS ARE GIVEN IN A SEPARATE PRICE LIST

R. E. DIETZ COMPANY - - - - - **NEW YORK, U. S. A.**

NO. 2 "WIZARD" WAGON LANTERN

REG. U. S. PAT. OFFICE—PATENTED

(COLD BLAST)

PACKED WITH
STYLE "E"
HOLDER

WILL TAKE
STYLE "B"
HOLDER

**DIETZ
NO. 2 "WIZARD"
WAGON LANTERN**

NO. 272 WING-LOCK BURNER
RISING CONE, 1″ WICK

MAGNIFYING LENS
ON PLATE

FOR KEROSENE

Made for left hand only

"D-LITE"
GLOBE

DOZ.

No. 2 Wizard Wagon Lanterns, Black Enamel . . . . .

R. E. DIETZ COMPANY - - - - - **NEW YORK, U. S. A.**

NO. 2 "WIZARD" WAGON LANTERN

REG. U. S. PAT. OFFICE—PATENTED

(COLD BLAST)

DIETZ NO. 2 "WIZARD" Wagon Lantern is large and gives a generous light on the road ahead. It is made for the left-hand side of the vehicle only.

The No. 2 "Wizard" complies with all night-driving laws, being equipped with a $2\frac{1}{4}$ inch ruby rear lens.

A combination holder permits the use of a round or flat bracket in fastening the Lantern in position on a vehicle. Nicely finished in Black Enamel.

Special features: DIETZ security standing bail, patent brass eyelets, patent safety (wing-lock) rising cone burner, patent reinforced tubes, patent globe lift on inside of frame, magnifying bullseye lens, ruby rear lens, combination holder, large oil-filler and double-seamed solderless dome-shaped oil fount with safety oil well.

SPECIFICATIONS

Height Over All	$13\frac{1}{4}$ Inches
Reflected Light by Test	20 C. Power
Size of Wick	1 Inch
Oil Used	150° Kerosene
Fount Capacity—Hours	18 Hours
Name of Globe	Dietz "D-Lite"
Patented Tinned Steel Burner (Rising Cone) . .	No. 272
Size of Magnifying Bullseye Lens	$2\frac{1}{4}$ Inches
Size of Ruby Rear Lens	$2\frac{1}{4}$ Inches
Quantity Packed in One Case	Half Dozen

PRICES, WEIGHTS AND MEASUREMENTS ARE GIVEN IN A SEPARATE PRICE LIST

R. E. DIETZ COMPANY - - - - - NEW YORK, U. S. A.

"EUREKA" DRIVING LANTERN

REG. U. S. PAT. OFFICE—PATENTED

WILL TAKE
STYLE "B"
HOLDER

PACKED WITH
STYLE "A"
HOLDER

DIETZ
"EUREKA"
DRIVING LANTERN

NO. 561 BURNER
LONG TUBE, 5/8 IN. WICK

2 1/4" RUBY
REAR LENS

FOR KEROSENE

Order for Right or Left Hand as Wanted

DOZ.

Eureka Driving Lanterns, Plain Lens, Black Enamel   .   .

Eureka Driving Lanterns, Optical Lens, Black Enamel   .   .

R. E. DIETZ COMPANY - - - - - **NEW YORK, U. S. A.**

"EUREKA" DRIVING LANTERN

REG. U. S. PAT. OFFICE—PATENTED

DIETZ "EUREKA" Driving Lantern is the smallest practical vehicle light made, being but 7¼ inches high.

No light carriage is complete without a pair of "Eurekas." The "Eureka" goes on any kind of vehicle and complies with all night-driving laws. It has a 2¼-inch ruby rear lens.

A bail permits the use of the "Eureka" as a Hand Lantern. Nicely finished in Black Enamel with nickel-plated door rim; plain or optical lens. Right and left hand.

Special features: Cold rolled steel body, patent long tube burner, positive-locking fount and large ruby rear lens.

SPECIFICATIONS

Height Over All	7¼ Inches
Reflected Light by Test	....
Size of Wick	⅝ Inch
Oil Used	150° Kerosene
Fount Capacity—Hours	10 Hours
Patented Tinned Steel Burner (Long Tube) . .	No. 561
Size of Door Lens	3⅛ Inches
Size of Ruby Lens	2¼ Inches
Quantity Packed in One Case	One Dozen

PRICES, WEIGHTS AND MEASUREMENTS ARE GIVEN IN A SEPARATE PRICE LIST

R. E. DIETZ COMPANY   -   -   -   -   -   NEW YORK, U. S. A.

"OCTO" DRIVING LANTERN

REG. U. S. PAT. OFFICE—PATENTED

(COLD BLAST)

WILL TAKE
STYLE "B"
HOLDER

PACKED WITH
STYLE "A"
HOLDER

DIETZ
"OCTO"
DRIVING LANTERN

NO. 510 BURNER
LONG CONE, 3/8" WICK

2 1/4" RUBY
REAR LENS

FOR KEROSENE

Double Sockets—For Right and Left Hand

	DOZ.
Octo Driving Lanterns, Plain Lens, Black Enamel . . .	
Octo Driving Lanterns, Optical Lens, Black Enamel . .	

R. E. DIETZ COMPANY - - - - - **NEW YORK, U. S. A.**

"OCTO" DRIVING LANTERN

REG. U S. PAT. OFFICE—PATENTED

(COLD BLAST)

Dietz "OCTO" Driving Lantern is of medium size, being 10¼ inches high.

The "Octo" is made with double sockets for right and left hand, with a 2¼-inch ruby rear lens. More pairs are sold than single Lanterns.

It complies with all night-driving laws. A bail permits its use as a Hand Lantern. Nicely finished in Black Enamel with nickel-plated door rim. Plain or optical lens.

Special features: Cold rolled steel body, patent long cone burner, positive-locking fount, large ruby rear lens.

SPECIFICATIONS

Height Over All	10¼ Inches
Reflected Light by Test	30 C. Power
Size of Wick	⅜ Inch
Oil Used	150° Kerosene
Fount Capacity—Hours	10 Hours
Nickel-plated Brass Burner (Long Cone)	No. 510
Size of Door Lens	4⅝ Inches
Size of Ruby Rear Lens	2¼ Inches
Quantity Packed in One Case	Half Dozen

PRICES, WEIGHTS AND MEASUREMENTS ARE GIVEN IN A SEPARATE PRICE LIST

R. E. DIETZ COMPANY - - - - - **NEW YORK, U. S. A.**

"UNION" DRIVING LANTERN

REG. U. S. PAT. OFFICE—PATENTED

(COLD BLAST)

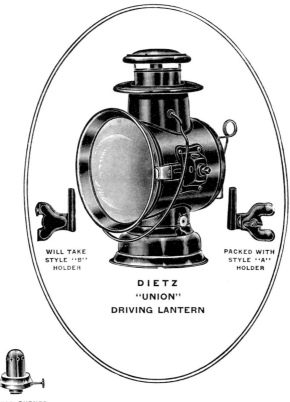

WILL TAKE
STYLE "B"
HOLDER

PACKED WITH
STYLE "A"
HOLDER

DIETZ
"UNION"
DRIVING LANTERN

NO. 510 BURNER
LONG CONE, 3/8 IN. WICK

2 1/4" RUBY
REAR LENS

FOR KEROSENE

Double Sockets—For Right and Left Hand

DOZ.

Union Driving Lanterns, Plain Lens, Black Enamel . .

Union Driving Lanterns, Optical Lens, Black Enamel . .

R. E. DIETZ COMPANY - - - - - **NEW YORK, U. S. A.**

"UNION" DRIVING LANTERN

REG. U. S. PAT. OFFICE—PATENTED

(COLD BLAST)

DIETZ "UNION" Driving Lantern is 11¼ inches high. It is the largest of the Dietz Driving Lanterns.

For more than 25 years this Lantern has been famous as a road illuminant. Thousands have been sold to country physicians who appreciate good light-giving quality on bad roads.

The "Union" complies with all night-driving laws. It is made with double sockets for right and left hand and a 2¼-inch ruby rear lens. A spring clip permits its use as a Dash Lantern and it has a hand bail. Nicely finished in Black Enamel with nickel-plated door rim. Plain or optical lens.

Special features: Cold rolled steel body, patent long cone burner, positive-locking fount, dash spring clip, large ruby rear lens.

SPECIFICATIONS

Height Over All	11¼ Inches
Reflected Light by Test	30 C. Power
Size of Wick	⅜ Inch
Oil Used	150° Kerosene
Fount Capacity—Hours	10 Hours
Nickel Plated Brass Burner (Long Cone) . . .	No. 510
Size of Door Lens	5 $^5/_{16}$ Inches
Size of Ruby Lens	2¼ Inches
Quantity Packed in One Case	Half Dozen

PRICES, WEIGHTS AND MEASUREMENTS ARE GIVEN IN A SEPARATE PRICE LIST

R. E. DIETZ COMPANY - - - - - **NEW YORK, U. S. A.**

"WATCHMAN'S" MILL LANTERN

(STEEL CLAD)

REG. U. S. PAT. OFFICE—PATENTED

DIETZ
"WATCHMAN'S"
MILL LANTERN
(STEEL CLAD)

NO. 652
WICK SCRAPER
RATCHET BURNER
1" WICK

"VULCAN"
GLOBE

FOR SIGNAL OIL

Watchman's Mill (Steel Clad) Lanterns, Red Enamel . .   *DOZ.*

R. E. DIETZ COMPANY - - - - - **NEW YORK, U. S. A.**

"WATCHMAN'S" MILL LANTERN

(STEEL CLAD)

REG. U. S. PAT. OFFICE—PATENTED

DIETZ "WATCHMAN'S" MILL (Steel Clad) Lantern, burning signal oil, is for use where kerosene is forbidden. It burns the same oil as the common types of Railroad Hand Lanterns.

To prevent a watchman tampering with the flame, the fount and globe are inserted through a hinged top which may be locked to the frame by a small padlock.

An outside wick raiser provides for the regulation of the flame and a wick scraper attachment removes the char. The Lantern is nicely finished in Red Enamel.

Special features: Cold rolled steel frame, inside fount, outside wick raiser and wick scraper combined.

SPECIFICATIONS

Height Over All	10¼ Inches
Volume of Light by Test	2 C. Power
Size of Wick	1 Inch
Oil Used	"Signal"
Fount Capacity—Hours	24 Hours
Name of Globe	Dietz "Vulcan"
Wick Scraper Ratchet Burner	No. 652
Quantity Packed in One Case	One Dozen

PRICES, WEIGHTS AND MEASUREMENTS ARE GIVEN IN A SEPARATE PRICE LIST

R. E. DIETZ COMPANY - - - - - **NEW YORK, U. S. A.**

"UNDERWRITER'S" MILL LANTERN

REG. U. S. PAT. OFFICE—PATENTED

APPROVED BY INSURANCE INSPECTION DEPARTMENT
(HOT BLAST)

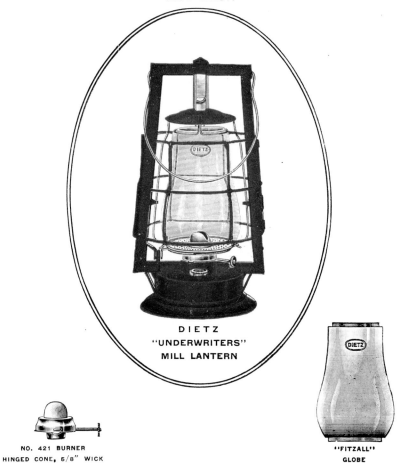

DIETZ
"UNDERWRITERS"
MILL LANTERN

NO. 421 BURNER
HINGED CONE, 5/8" WICK

"FITZALL"
GLOBE

FOR KEROSENE

DOZ.

Underwriter's Mill Lanterns, Red Enamel . . . .

R. E. DIETZ COMPANY - - - - - NEW YORK, U. S. A.

"UNDERWRITER'S" MILL LANTERN

REG. U. S. PAT. OFFICE—PATENTED
APPROVED BY INSURANCE INSPECTION DEPARTMENT
(HOT BLAST)

DIETZ "UNDERWRITER'S" Mill Lantern is light in weight but strongly built and guarded.

Requirements of the Insurance Inspection Department are strictly followed. The hinged guard may be padlocked, preventing access to the flame, and a safety oil well is provided.

Mill Supply Houses find the Dietz special types of Locked Mill Lanterns a profitable line to push. The "Underwriter's" is nicely finished in Red Enamel.

Special features: DIETZ security standing bail, patent brass eyelets, patent hinged-cone burner, large oil-filler, hinged wire locking guard, braced frame and safety oil well.

SPECIFICATIONS

Height Over All	$13\frac{1}{4}$ Inches
Volume of Light by Test	4 C. Power
Size of Wick	$\frac{5}{8}$ Inch
Oil Used	150° Kerosene
Fount Capacity—Hours	23 Hours
Name of Globe	Dietz "Fitzall"
Patented Tinned Steel Burner (Hinged Cone)	No. 421
Quantity Packed in One Case	One Dozen

PRICES, WEIGHTS AND MEASUREMENTS ARE GIVEN IN A SEPARATE PRICE LIST

R. E. DIETZ COMPANY - - - - - **NEW YORK, U S. A.**

NO. 2 "BLIZZARD" MILL LANTERN

REG. U. S. PAT. OFFICE—PATENTED

APPROVED BY INSURANCE INSPECTION DEPARTMENT
(COLD BLAST)

**DIETZ
NO. 2 "BLIZZARD"
MILL LANTERN**

**NO. 252 BURNER
SLOTTED CONE 1″ WICK**

**"BLIZZARD"
GLOBE**

FOR KEROSENE

DOZ.

No. 2 Blizzard Mill Lanterns, Red Enamel . . . .

R. E. DIETZ COMPANY - - - - - **NEW YORK, U. S. A.**

NO. 2 "BLIZZARD" MILL LANTERN

REG. U. S. PAT. OFFICE—PATENTED

APPROVED BY INSURANCE INSPECTION DEPARTMENT

(COLD BLAST)

DIETZ NO. 2 "BLIZZARD" Mill Lantern gives a light of ten candle-power. The exacting requirements of the Insurance Inspection Department are incorporated in this Lantern to the last detail and it may be padlocked to prevent access to the flame.

As a general purpose Lantern for use in making night repairs to machinery, etc., where other illumination is cut off, and around construction work, this Lantern is invaluable. Nicely finished in Red Enamel.

Special features: DIETZ security standing bail, patent brass eyelets, patent slotted cone burner, patent reinforced tubes, patent globe-lift on inside of frame, fount strongly braced, large oil-filler, safety oil well and double-seamed solderless oil fount.

SPECIFICATIONS

Height Over All	14¾ Inches
Reflected Light by Test	10 C. Power
Size of Wick	1 Inch
Oil Used	150° Kerosene
Fount Capacity—Hours	18 Hours
Name of Globe	Dietz"Blizzard"
Patented Tinned Steel Burner (Slotted Cone)	No. 252
Quantity Packed in One Case	Half Dozen

PRICES, WEIGHTS AND MEASUREMENTS ARE GIVEN IN A SEPARATE PRICE LIST

R. E. DIETZ COMPANY - - - - - NEW YORK, U. S. A.

"KING" FIRE DEP'T LANTERN

REG. U. S. PAT. OFFICE—PATENTED

(HOT BLAST)

DIETZ
"KING" FIRE DEP'T
LANTERN

NO. 421 BURNER
HINGED CONE, 5/8" WICK

"FITZALL"
HEAT-RESISTING
GLOBE

DIETZ
"KING" FIRE DEP'T
LANTERN
WITH GUARD RAISED
(BRASS)

FOR KEROSENE

DOZ.

King Fire Dep't Lanterns, Red Enamel, Copper Fount . .
King Fire Dep't Lanterns, Nickel-plated on Tin, Copper Fount .
King Fire Dep't Lanterns, Polished Brass . . . . .
King Fire Dep't Lanterns, Nickel-plated on Brass . . .

R. E. DIETZ COMPANY - - - - - NEW YORK, U. S. A.

"KING" FIRE DEP'T LANTERN

REG. U. S. PAT. OFFICE—PATENTED

(HOT BLAST)

DIETZ "KING" FIRE DEPARTMENT Lantern has been the Standard of Fire Departments and Insurance Patrols for over two decades.

No modern motor or horse-drawn fire apparatus is complete without one or more of Dietz oil-burning Fire Department Lanterns.

The "King" Lantern is heavily constructed and will burn in all situations where there is air to support human life. It is finely finished and equipped with heat-resisting globes. Fits any standard bracket.

Special features: DIETZ reinforced bail, apparatus hook, patent hinged-cone burner, patent hinged wind and water guard, steel-lined oil fount with safety oil well and large oil-filler.

SPECIFICATIONS

Height Over All	14½ Inches
Volume of Light by Test	4 C. Power
Size of Wick	⅝ Inch
Oil Used	150° Kerosene
Fount Capacity—Hours	13 Hours
Name of Heat-Resisting Globe (White, Ruby, Blue and Green)	Dietz"Fitzall"
Patented Tinned Steel Burner (Hinged Cone)	No. 421
Quantity Packed in One Case	One Dozen

PRICES, WEIGHTS AND MEASUREMENTS ARE GIVEN IN A SEPARATE PRICE LIST

R. E. DIETZ COMPANY   -   -   -   -   -   NEW YORK, U. S. A.

NO. 2
"WIZARD" FIRE DEP'T LANTERN

REG. U. S. PAT. OFFICE—PATENTED

(COLD BLAST)

**DIETZ
"WIZARD" FIRE DEP'T
LANTERN**

NO. 272 WING-LOCK BURNER
RISING CONE, 1" WICK

"D-LITE"
HEAT-RESISTING
GLOBE

**DIETZ
"WIZARD" FIRE DEP'T
LANTERN**
WITH GUARD RAISED
(BRASS)

FOR KEROSENE

DOZ.

No. 2 Wizard Fire Dep't Lanterns, Red Enamel and Brass Fount
No. 2 Wizard Fire Dep't Lanterns, Polished Brass . . .
No. 2 Wizard Fire Dep't Lanterns, Nickel-plated on Brass . .

R. E. DIETZ COMPANY - - - - - NEW YORK, U. S. A.

NO. 2
"WIZARD" FIRE DEP'T LANTERN

REG. U. S. PAT. OFFICE—PATENTED

(COLD BLAST)

DIETZ NO. 2 "WIZARD" FIRE DEPARTMENT Lantern is new. It is the first Lantern for Fire Department use on the market built on the Cold Blast principle and with a Short Globe.

The "Wizard" may be had in Bright Tin with Brass Fount, all Brass, and Nickel-Plated, with heat-resisting globes.

This new and excellent Lantern is strongly made, easily cleaned, filled and lighted, and will burn where there is air to support human life. Fits any standard bracket.

Special features: DIETZ patent safety (winglock) rising cone burner, patent reinforced tubes, large oil filler, patented guard, and double-seamed solderless, dome-shaped oil fount.

SPECIFICATIONS

Height Over All	14¾ Inches
Volume of Light by Test	10 C. Power
Size of Wick	1 Inch
Oil Used	150° Kerosene
Fount Capacity—Hours	16 Hours
Name of Heat Resisting Globe (White, Ruby, Blue and Green)	Dietz "D-Lite"
Patented Tinned Steel Burner (Rising Cone) . .	No. 272
Quantity Packed in One Case	Half Dozen

PRICES, WEIGHTS AND MEASUREMENTS ARE GIVEN IN A SEPARATE PRICE LIST

R. E. DIETZ COMPANY - - - - - **NEW YORK, U. S. A.**

NO.'S 15 AND 25 WALL LANTERNS

REG. U. S. PAT. OFFICE—PATENTED

(COLD BLAST)

**DIETZ
WALL LANTERNS**
TWO SIZES
NO.'S 15 AND 25

"FITZALL"
GLOBE

NO. 221
BURNER

NO. 262
BURNER

"BLIZZARD"
GLOBE

NO. 15 TAKES NO. 221 BURNER 5/8" WICK
NO. 25 TAKES NO. 262 BURNER 1" WICK

NO. 15 TAKES "FITZALL" GLOBE
NO. 25 TAKES "BLIZZARD" GLOBE

6" SILVERED REFLECTOR

FOR KEROSENE

	DOZ.
No. 15 Wall Lanterns, Green Enamel	
No. 25 Wall Lanterns, Green Enamel	

R. E. DIETZ COMPANY - - - - - **NEW YORK, U. S. A.**

NO.'S 15 AND 25 WALL LANTERNS

REG. U. S. PAT. OFFICE—PATENTED

(COLD BLAST)

DIETZ NO.'S 15 AND 25 Wall Lanterns are useful indoors and out. They give a big reflected light.

For cellarways, dark passages, stairways, sheds, outhouses and similar places these Lanterns have no equal. One will easily light a small room.

The globe lifts clear of the Burner to permit trimming and lighting. Filling is done through an outside filler cap. Nicely finished in Green Enamel.

These Wall Lanterns are not intended for use as portable Lanterns or vehicle lights.

SPECIFICATIONS

	NO. 15 SIZE	NO. 25 SIZE
Height Over All	15 Inches	15 Inches
Reflected Light by Test . . .	20 C. Power	30 C. Power
Size of Wick	5/8 Inch	1 Inch
Oil Used	150° Kerosene	150° Kerosene
Fount Capacity—Hours . . .	45 Hours	35 Hours
Name of Globe (White only) . .	Dietz"Fitzall"	Dietz"Blizzard"
Patented Tinned Steel Burner .	No. 221	No. 262
Size of Silvered Glass Reflector . .	5 Inches	6 Inches
Quantity Packed in One Case . .	Half Dozen	Half Dozen

PRICES, WEIGHTS AND MEASUREMENTS ARE GIVEN IN A SEPARATE PRICE LIST

R. E. DIETZ COMPANY - - - - - NEW YORK, U. S. A.

"BEACON" WALL LANTERNS

REG. U. S. PAT. OFFICE—PATENTED

(COLD BLAST)

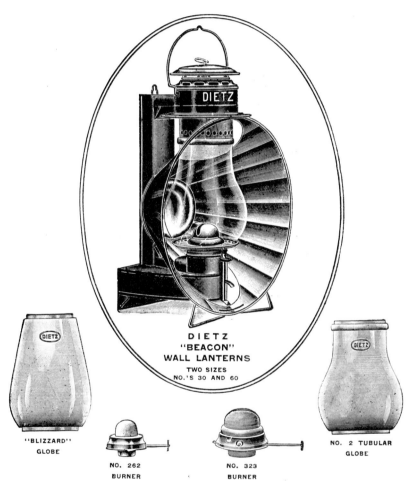

DIETZ
"BEACON"
WALL LANTERNS
TWO SIZES
NO.'S 30 AND 60

"BLIZZARD"
GLOBE

NO. 262
BURNER

NO. 323
BURNER

NO. 2 TUBULAR
GLOBE

NO. 30 TAKES NO. 262 BURNER 1" WICK
NO. 60 TAKES NO. 323 BURNER 1/2" WICK

NO. 30 TAKES "BLIZZARD" GLOBE
NO. 60 TAKES NO. 2 TUBULAR GLOBE

FOR KEROSENE

DOZ.

No. 30 Beacon Wall Lanterns, Green Enamel . . . . .

No. 60 Beacon Wall Lanterns, Green Enamel . . . . .

R. E. DIETZ COMPANY - - - - - NEW YORK, U. S A.

"BEACON" WALL LANTERNS

REG. U. S. PAT. OFFICE—PATENTED

(COLD BLAST)

DIETZ "BEACON" Wall Lanterns (two sizes) are equipped with large fluted reflectors and are powerful light-givers.

They are especially suitable for the lighting of dancing platforms, boat landings, horse sheds, open air meetings, etc., etc.

The globe lifts clear of the burner to permit trimming and lighting. Filling is done through an outside filler cap. Nicely finished in Green Enamel.

These Wall Lanterns are not intended for use as portable Lanterns or vehicle lights.

SPECIFICATIONS

	NO. 30 SIZE	NO. 60 SIZE
Height Over All . . .	15¼ Inches	20½ Inches
Reflected Light by Test . .	50 C. Power	100 C. Power
Size of Wick	1 Inch	1½ Inches
Oil Used	150° Kerosene	150° Kerosene
Fount Capacity—Hours . .	35 Hours	30 Hours
Name of Globe (White only) .	Dietz"Blizzard"	Dietz No. 2 Tubular
Patent Tinned Steel Burner .	No. 262	No. 323
Size of Bullseye Lens (No. 30 Only)	2¼ Inches	. . . .
Size of Reflector (No. 60 Only) .	. . . .	5 Inches
Quantity Packed in One Case .	Quarter Dozen	One Only

PRICES, WEIGHTS AND MEASUREMENTS ARE GIVEN IN A SEPARATE PRICE LIST

R. E. DIETZ COMPANY   -   -   -   -   -   NEW YORK, U. S. A.

"PIONEER" STREET LANTERN

REG. U. S. PAT. OFFICE—PATENTED

(COLD BLAST)

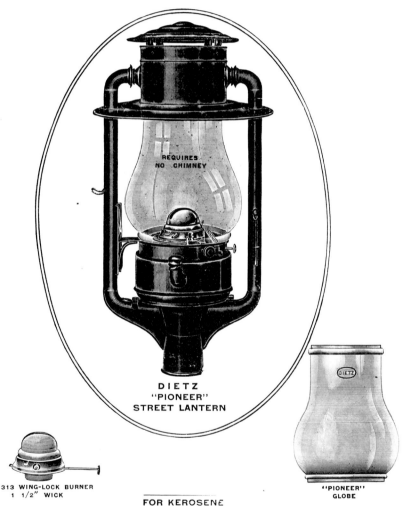

REQUIRES NO CHIMNEY

DIETZ
"PIONEER"
STREET LANTERN

NO. 313 WING-LOCK BURNER
1 1/2" WICK

"PIONEER"
GLOBE

FOR KEROSENE

EACH

Pioneer Street Lanterns, Green Enamel . . . . .
Pioneer Street Lanterns, Glass Fount . . . . .
Pioneer Street Lanterns, Brass Fount . . . . .
Pioneer Street Lanterns, All Brass, Green Enamel . . .

R. E. DIETZ COMPANY - - - - - **NEW YORK, U. S. A.**

"PIONEER" STREET LANTERN

REG. U. S. PAT. OFFICE—PATENTED

(COLD BLAST)

DIETZ "PIONEER" Street Lantern is the standard of the United States Government, and many Railway systems use it extensively as a Platform Lantern.

There is nothing like the "Pioneer" for use in situations where gas or electricity are impossible. It gives double the light of a common Street Lamp (gas), may be filled lighted and regulated from the outside, and is self-extinguishing.

The "Pioneer" has been on the market for over three decades and the sales increase yearly. It is used for village lighting more and more, and thousands are sold for door yard lighting and similar uses.

For damp or exposed situations the all-brass Lantern or one with a brass fount is recommended. Well finished in Green Enamel.

SPECIFICATIONS

Height Over All	25½ Inches
Volume of Light by Test	22 C. Power
Size of Wick	1½ Inches
Oil Used	150° Kerosene
Fount Capacity—Hours	24 Hours
Name of Globe (White, Ruby, Blue and Green) . .	Dietz "Pioneer"
Patented Tinned Steel Burner (Wing-lock) . .	No. 313
Size of Post Socket Opening	2⅞ Inches
Quantity Packed in One Case	One or Two

PRICES, WEIGHTS AND MEASUREMENTS ARE GIVEN IN A SEPARATE PRICE LIST

R. E. DIETZ COMPANY - - - - - **NEW YORK, U. S. A.**

"PIONEER" HANGING LANTERN

REG. U. S. PAT. OFFICE—PATENTED

(COLD BLAST)

DIETZ
"PIONEER"
HANGING LANTERN

NO. 313 WING-LOCK BURNER
1 1/2" WICK

FOR KEROSENE

"PIONEER"
GLOBE

EACH

Pioneer Hanging Lanterns, Green Enamel . . . .

Pioneer Hanging Lanterns, Glass Fount . . . . .

Pioneer Hanging Lanterns, Brass Fount . . . . .

R. E. DIETZ COMPANY - - - - - **NEW YORK, U. S. A.**

"PIONEER" HANGING LANTERN

REG. U. S. PAT. OFFICE—PATENTED

(COLD BLAST)

DIETZ "PIONEER" Hanging Lantern has a stamped base and a substantial bail.

Many subways and tunnels employ this Hanging Lantern as an emergency light. It is useful everywhere and gives twice the light of a common Street Lamp (gas); may be filled, lighted and regulated from the outside and is self-extinguishing.

There is a good profit in the sale of "Pioneer" Lanterns and a surprising number are sold by Dealers who keep a sample Lantern in a conspicuous place.

For damp or exposed situations the Lantern with a brass fount is recommended. Well finished in Green Enamel.

SPECIFICATIONS

Height Over All	21½ Inches
Volume of Light by Test	22 C. Power
Size of Wick	1½ Inches
Oil Used	150° Kerosene
Fount Capacity—Hours	24 Hours
Name of Globe (White, Ruby, Blue and Green)	Dietz "Pioneer"
Patented Tinned Steel Burner (Wing-lock)	No. 313
Quantity Packed in One Case	One

PRICES, WEIGHTS AND MEASUREMENTS ARE GIVEN IN A SEPARATE PRICE LIST

R. E. DIETZ COMPANY - - - - - NEW YORK, U. S. A

"IMPERIAL" PLATFORM LANTERN

REG. U. S. PAT. OFFICE—PATENTED

(COLD BLAST)

DIETZ
"IMPERIAL"
PLATFORM LANTERN

NO. 303 WING-LOCK BURNER
1 1/2" WICK

8" SILVERED
REFLECTOR

FOR KEROSENE

Imperial Platform Lantern, Green Enamel . . . . *EACH*

R. E. DIETZ COMPANY - - - - - - NEW YORK, U. S. A.

"IMPERIAL" PLATFORM LANTERN

REG. U. S. PAT. OFFICE—PATENTED

(COLD BLAST)

Dietz "IMPERIAL" Platform Lantern with its Cold Blast system of air supply is unique among Lanterns of its class.

No other Platform Lantern equals the "Imperial" in the remarkable volume of steady reflected light, and the freedom from care in its operation.

The "Imperial" is largely used by Railroads both as a Platform and Station Lantern. For all phases of outdoor and indoor lighting where a big safe light is required, this Lantern is unexcelled. Well finished in Green Enamel.

SPECIFICATIONS

Height Over All	21 Inches
Extreme Width	10½ "
Extreme Depth	10¼ "
Reflected Light by Test	100 C. Power
Size of Wick	1½ Inches
Oil Used	150° Kerosene
Fount Capacity—Hours	17 Hours
Patented Tinned Steel Burner (Wing-lock) . .	No. 303
Size of Silvered Glass Reflector	8 Inches
Quantity Packed in One Case	One

PRICES, WEIGHTS AND MEASUREMENTS ARE GIVEN IN A SEPARATE PRICE LIST

R. E. DIETZ COMPANY - - - - - NEW YORK, U. S. A.

"CLIMAX" PLATFORM LANTERN

REG. U. S. PAT. OFFICE—PATENTED

DIETZ
"CLIMAX"
PLATFORM LANTERNS
TWO SIZES
NO.'S 1 AND 2

NO.'S 111 AND 162
CHIMNEY BURNERS

REFLECTOR

SUN BULB
CHIMNEY

NO. 1 TAKES NO. 111 BURNER, 5/8" WICK, NO. 1 CHIMNEY AND 7" REFLECTOR
NO. 2 TAKES NO. 162 BURNER, 1" WICK, NO. 2 CHIMNEY AND 8" REFLECTOR

FOR KEROSENE

EACH

No. 1 Climax Platform Lanterns, Green Enamel . . .
No. 2 Climax Platform Lanterns, Green Enamel . . .

R. E. DIETZ COMPANY - - - - **NEW YORK, U. S. A.**

"CLIMAX" PLATFORM LANTERN

REG. U. S. PAT. OFFICE—PATENTED

DIETZ "CLIMAX" Platform Lanterns (two sizes) are of simple design and moderate candle power.

A well made metal box frame with window glass on three sides and a ventilating top, contains a substantial Metal Lamp with a Sun Bulb chimney and a silvered glass reflector.

"Climax" Lanterns are used indoors and outdoors where a powerful light is not needed. They are inexpensive and handy. Well finished in Green Enamel.

SPECIFICATIONS

	SIZE NO. 1	SIZE NO. 2
Height Over All	15 Inches	17½ Inches
Extreme Width	8¾ "	10¼ "
Extreme Depth	7⅜ "	8¾ "
Reflected Light by Test . . .	. . . .	. . . .
Size of Wick	⅝ Inch	1 Inch
Oil Used	150° Kerosene	150° Kerosene
Fount Capacity—Hours . . .	20 Hours	23 Hours
Burner	No. 111	No. 162
Chimney	No. 1 Sunbulb	No. 2 Sunbulb
Size of Silvered Glass Reflector . .	7 Inches	8 Inches
Quantity Packed in One Case . .	One	One

NOTE—*The two sizes may be bought nested in one case, complete with Founts, etc.*

PRICES, WEIGHTS AND MEASUREMENTS ARE GIVEN IN A SEPARATE PRICE LIST

R. E. DIETZ COMPANY - - - - - NEW YORK, U. S. A.

"U. S." LANTERN

REG. U. S. PAT. OFFICE—PATENTED

DIETZ
"U. S." LANTERN

NO. 371 BURNER
5/8" WICK

LITTLE STAR U. S.
GLOBE

FOR KEROSENE

DOZ.

U. S. Lanterns, Bright Tin . . . .

R. E. DIETZ COMPANY - - - - - **NEW YORK, U. S. A.**

"U. S." LANTERN

REG. U. S. PAT. OFFICE—PATENTED

DIETZ "U. S." is a practical and inexpensive Lantern without side tubes, and equipped with a Convex burner.

For parades and night illuminations, the "U. S." is most adaptable, and affords pleasing variety by the use of colored globes.

Considerable numbers of this handy and low-priced Lantern are shipped to all parts of the world.

SPECIFICATIONS

Height Over All	. 10 Inches
Volume of Light by Test	. 2 C. Power
Size of Wick	. ⅝ Inch
Oil Used	. 150° Kerosene
Fount Capacity—Hours	. 14 Hours
Name of Globe (White, Ruby, Blue and Green) .	Dietz "Little Star U.S."
Name of Special Convex Burner . .	. No. 371
Quantity Packed in One Case (assorted) .	. Two Dozen

PRICES, WEIGHTS AND MEASUREMENTS ARE GIVEN IN A SEPARATE PRICE LIST

R. E. DIETZ COMPANY - - - - NEW YORK, U. S. A.

"A No. ONE" LANTERN

REG. U. S. PAT. OFFICE—PATENTED

DIETZ
" A NO. ONE" LANTERN

NO. 351 BURNER
5/8" WICK

"FITZALL"
GLOBE

FOR KEROSENE

DOZ.

A No. One Lanterns, Bright Tin .   .   .   .

R. E. DIETZ COMPANY -   -   -   -   -   **NEW YORK, U. S. A.**

"A No. ONE" LANTERN

REG. U. S. PAT. OFFICE—PATENTED

DIETZ "A No. ONE" Lantern has been on the market for over 35 years. It is of the semi-railroad type and equipped with convex burner to burn kerosene.

No simpler Lantern is made. The globe is removed through the frame by turning back the hinged top, and the oil fount is held in place by Sangster springs and drops out through the bottom.

The "A No. One" is very popular in Foreign countries, large quantities being exported annually.

SPECIFICATIONS

Height Over All	10¾ Inches
Volume of Light by Test	2 C. Power
Size of Wick	⅝ Inch
Oil Used	150° Kerosene
Fount Capacity—Hours	15 Hours
Name of Globe (White, Ruby and Green) . . .	Dietz "Fitzall"
Tinned Steel Convex Burner	No. 351
Quantity Packed in One Case	One Dozen

PRICES, WEIGHTS AND MEASUREMENTS ARE GIVEN IN A SEPARATE PRICE LIST

R. E. DIETZ COMPANY   -   -   -   -   -   NEW YORK, U. S. A.

"POLICE" LANTERN

WITH BULLSEYE LENS

REG. U. S. PAT. OFFICE—PATENTED

DIETZ
POLICE LANTERN
WITH BULLS-EYE LENS

NO. 601 BURNER
5/8" WICK

3" MAGNIFYING
BULLSEYE LENS

FOR SIGNAL OIL

DOZ.

Police Lanterns, Brown Japan .   .   .   .

R. E. DIETZ COMPANY - - - - - **NEW YORK, U. S. A.**

"POLICE" LANTERN

WITH BULLSEYE LENS

REG. U. S. PAT. OFFICE—PATENTED

DIETZ "POLICE" Lantern is 8 inches high, burns Signal Oil (a mixture of heavy animal or vegetable oils and kerosene) and gives a strong beam of light through a 3-inch magnifying bullseye lens.

The Lantern may be carried in the hand or attached to a belt by a spring clip. A cut-off slide behind the bullseye is operated backward or forward by the thumb of the supporting hand.

This type of "Police" Lantern is known as the "Flash" through the operator's ability to throw a beam of light or cut it off at will.

SPECIFICATIONS

Height Over All	8 Inches
Volume of Reflected Light	3 C. Power
Size of Wick	⅝ Inch
Oil Used	"Signal"
Fount Capacity—Hours	16 Hours
Name of Special Ratchet Burner	No. 601
Size of Bullseye Lens	3 Inches
Quantity Packed in One Case	Two Dozen

PRICES, WEIGHTS AND MEASUREMENTS ARE GIVEN IN A SEPARATE PRICE LIST

R. E. DIETZ COMPANY - - - - - **NEW YORK, U. S. A.**

TRAFFIC SIGNAL LANTERN

WITH RUBY AND GREEN LENSES

REG. U. S. PAT. OFFICE—PATENTED

TRAFFIC SIGNAL LANTERN
(ONE-HALF SIZE)

DOZ.

Traffic Signal Lanterns, Black Enamel . . . . . .

R. E. DIETZ COMPANY - - - - - **NEW YORK, U. S. A.**

TRAFFIC SIGNAL LANTERN
WITH RUBY AND GREEN LENSES
REG. U. S. PAT. OFFICE—PATENTED

DIETZ TRAFFIC SIGNAL Lantern is small and compact, but highly efficient.

It is about 8½ inches high, and its equipment consists of two ruby and two green 3½ inch lenses, lighted by a long time burner. The fount is of the inside type and cannot be lost off.

This Lantern may be used with the "Go—Stop" traffic signals governing street traffic, or in connection with railroad crossing gates, etc., etc.

SPECIFICATIONS

Height Over All	8½ Inches
Volume of Light by Test	. . . .
Size of Wick	. . . .
Oil Used	150° Kerosene
Fount Capacity—Hours	. . . .
Size of Ruby and Green Lenses	3½ Inches
Style of Burner	Long Time
Quantity Packed in One Case	1 Dozen

PRICES, WEIGHTS AND MEASUREMENTS ARE GIVEN IN A SEPARATE PRICE LIST

R. E. DIETZ COMPANY - - - - - **NEW YORK, U. S. A.**

"STANDARD" (NO. 39) RAILROAD LANTERN

WITH WING-LOCK RATCHET BURNER

REG. U. S. PAT. OFFICE—PATENTED

DIETZ
"STANDARD"
R. R. LANTERN

NO. 2 WING-LOCK
RATCHET BURNER
1″ WICK

"VULCAN"
(NO. 39) GLOBE

FOR SIGNAL OIL

	DOZ.
Standard Railroad Lanterns, Bright Tin	

R. E. DIETZ COMPANY - - - - - NEW YORK, U. S. A

"STANDARD" (NO. 39) RAILROAD LANTERN

WITH WING-LOCK RATCHET BURNER

REG. U. S. PAT. OFFICE—PATENTED

DIETZ "STANDARD" (No. 39) Railroad Lantern with patented wing-lock ratchet burner, is made with a double guard and a substantial stamped base and top.

The globe is removed through the frame by turning back the hinged top. The wing-lock (slip collar) burner is firmly attached to the fount by patented locking lugs and the base containing the fount fastens to the frame by a patented positive-locking device operated by a twist of the hand. Fount has a safety oil well.

For strength and long life, ease in cleaning, filling, lighting and regulating (outside wick raiser), and dependability in making signals, Dietz No. 39 Lanterns are unexcelled.

No. 1 or No. 2 slip collar wing-lock ratchet burners. Collar will take Dietz No. 1 wing-lock convex burner for kerosene.

SPECIFICATIONS

Height Over All	10 Inches
Volume of Light by Test	2 C. Power
Size of Wick	1 Inch
Oil Used	"Signal"
Fount Capacity—Hours	24 Hours
Name of Globe (White, Ruby, Blue and Green)	Dietz"Vulcan"(No. 39)
*Regular Burner	No. 2 "Winglock" Rat.
Quantity Packed in Cases for Jobbing Trade	One Dozen

*For Kerosene, Substitute No. 1 "Winglock" Convex Burner.

PRICES, WEIGHTS AND MEASUREMENTS ARE GIVEN IN A SEPARATE PRICE LIST

R. E. DIETZ COMPANY   -   -   -   -   -   NEW YORK, U. S. A.

"VULCAN" (NO. 39) RAILROAD LANTERN

WITH WING-LOCK RATCHET BURNER

REG. U. S. PAT. OFFICE—PATENTED

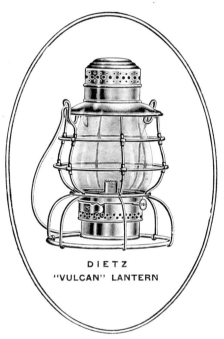

DIETZ
"VULCAN" LANTERN

NO. 2 WING-LOCK
RATCHET BURNER
1" WICK

"VULCAN"
(NO. 39) GLOBE

___

FOR SIGNAL OIL

___

DOZ.

Vulcan Railroad Lanterns. Bright Tin . . . . .

___

R. E. DIETZ COMPANY -   -   -   -   - NEW YORK, U. S. A.

"VULCAN" (NO. 39) RAILROAD LANTERN

WITH WING-LOCK RATCHET BURNER

REG. U. S. PAT. OFFICE—PATENTED

DIETZ "VULCAN" (No. 39) Railroad Lantern with patented wing-lock ratchet burner is made with a strong wire frame, double guard, and stamped fount and top.

The globe is removed through the frame by turning back the hinged top. The wing-lock (slip collar) burner is firmly attached to the fount by patented locking lugs and the fount fastens to the frame by a patented positive-locking device operated by a twist of the hand. Fount has a safety oil well.

For strength and long life, ease in cleaning, filling, lighting and regulating (outside wick raiser) and dependability in making signals, Dietz No. 39 Lanterns are unexcelled.

No. 1 or No. 2 slip collar wing-lock ratchet burners. Collar will take Dietz No. 1 wing-lock convex burner for kerosene.

SPECIFICATIONS

Height Over All	10 Inches
Volume of Light by Test	2 C. Power
Size of Wick	1 Inch
Oil Used	"Signal"
Fount Capacity—Hours	24 Hours
Name of Globe (White, Ruby, Blue and Green)	Dietz"Vulcan"(No. 39)
*Regular Burner	No. 2 "Winglock" Rat.
Quantity Packed in Cases for Jobbing Trade	One Dozen

*For Kerosene, Substitute No. 1 "Winglock" Convex Burner.

PRICES, WEIGHTS AND MEASUREMENTS ARE GIVEN IN A SEPARATE PRICE LIST

R. E. DIETZ COMPANY - - - - - **NEW YORK, U. S. A.**

"STEEL CLAD" (NO. 39) RAILROAD LANTERN

WITH WING-LOCK RATCHET BURNER

REG. U. S. PAT. OFFICE—PATENTED

**DIETZ
"STEEL CLAD"
LANTERN**

NO. 2 WING-LOCK
RATCHET BURNER
1″ WICK

"VULCAN"
(NO. 39) GLOBE

FOR SIGNAL OIL

DOZ.

Steel Clad Lanterns, Bright Tin . . . . . .

R. E. DIETZ COMPANY -   -   -   -   -   NEW YORK, U. S. A.

"STEEL CLAD" (NO. 39) RAILROAD LANTERN

WITH WING-LOCK RATCHET BURNER

REG. U. S. PAT. OFFICE—PATENTED

DIETZ "STEEL CLAD" (No. 39) Railroad Lantern with patented wing-lock ratchet burner is made with a frame of stamped steel with a double wire guard, and stamped fount and top.

The globe is removed through the frame by turning back the hinged top. The wing-lock (slip collar) burner is firmly attached to the fount by patented locking lugs and the fount fastens to the frame by a patented positive-locking device operated by a twist of the hand. Fount has a safety oil well.

For strength and long life, ease in cleaning, filling, lighting and regulating (outside wick raiser) and dependability in making signals, Dietz No. 39 Lanterns are unexcelled.

No. 1 or No. 2 slip collar wing-lock ratchet burners. Collar will take Dietz No. 1 wing-lock convex burner for kerosene.

SPECIFICATIONS

Height Over All	10 Inches
Volume of Light by Test	2 C. Power
Size of Wick	1 Inch
Oil Used	"Signal"
Fount Capacity—Hours	24 Hours
Name of Globe (White, Ruby, Blue and Green)	Dietz "Vulcan" (No. 39)
*Regular Burner	No. 2 "Winglock" Rat.
Quantity Packed in Cases for Jobbing Trade	One Dozen

*For Kerosene, Substitute No. 1 "Winglock" Convex Burner.

PRICES, WEIGHTS AND MEASUREMENTS ARE GIVEN IN A SEPARATE PRICE LIST

R. E. DIETZ COMPANY - - - - - - **NEW YORK, U S A.**

"NO. 6" RAILROAD LANTERN

NEW YORK CENTRAL STYLE

REG. U. S. PAT. OFFICE—PATENTED

DIETZ
"NO. 6"
R. R. LANTERN

NO. 2 SCREW COLLAR
RATCHET BURNER
1" WICK

"NO. 6"
GLOBE

FOR SIGNAL OIL

No. 6 Railroad Lanterns, Bright Tin . . . . . .   *DOZ.*

R. E. DIETZ COMPANY - - - - - **NEW YORK, U. S. A.**

"NO. 6" RAILROAD LANTERN

NEW YORK CENTRAL STYLE

REG. U. S. PAT. OFFICE—PATENTED

DIETZ "NO. 6" Railroad Lantern (New York Central style) has been on the market over 30 years and been used by the New York Central System during all of that time.

The "No. 6" is special in that it takes its own (No. 6) globe and will not interchange with Lanterns taking the ordinary (No. 39) Railroad globe.

The globe is removed through the frame by turning back the hinged top. The fount locks within the Lantern body by Sangster springs and is fitted with a screw collar burner.

No. 1 or No. 2 screw collar ratchet burners. Collar will take a Kerosene (convex) screw burner.

SPECIFICATIONS

Height Over All	10 Inches
Volume of Light by Test	2 C. Power
Size of Wick (No. 1 Burner)	1 Inch
Oil Used	"Signal"
Fount Capacity—Hours	15 Hours
Name of Globe (White, Ruby, Blue and Green) . .	Dietz " No. 6"
Regular Burner	No. 2 Ratchet
Quantity Packed in Cases for Jobbing Trade . .	One Dozen

PRICES, WEIGHTS AND MEASUREMENTS ARE GIVEN IN A SEPARATE PRICE LIST

R. E. DIETZ COMPANY - - - - - NEW YORK, U. S. A.

"X L C R" SWITCHMAN'S LANTERN

WITH WING-LOCK RATCHET BURNER

REG. U. S. PAT. OFFICE—PATENTED

DIETZ
X L C R
SWITCHMAN'S LANTERN
ADJUSTABLE INSULATED BAIL
AND OUTSIDE WICK RAISER

NO. 2 WING-LOCK
RATCHET BURNER
1″ WICK

"VULCAN"
(NO. 39) GLOBE

FOR SIGNAL OIL

DOZ.

X L C R Switchman's Lanterns, Bright Tin . . . .

R. E. DIETZ COMPANY - - - - - **NEW YORK, U. S. A.**

"X L C R" SWITCHMAN'S LANTERN

WITH WING-LOCK RATCHET-BURNER

REG. U. S. PAT. OFFICE—PATENTED

DIETZ "X L C R" Switchman's Lantern is small and compact, being but 9 inches high.

The "X L C R" is a tried and proven Lantern for its special purpose.   It has an insulated fibre bail which can be locked into a stiff bail for signalling, and a wing-lock (slip collar) burner attached to the fount by patented lugs and taking a 1-inch wick.   Fount has a safety oil well.

No other Switchman's Lantern is so light in weight or so easy to clean, fill, light and regulate (outside wick raiser), or so dependable in making signals.

Where Electric traction is employed, the insulated bail of the "X L C R" will prevent a deadly shock through accidental contact with the third rail.

SPECIFICATIONS

Height Over All	9 Inches
Volume of Light by Test	2 C. Power
Size of Wick	1 Inch
Oil Used	"Signal"
Fount Capacity—Hours	24 Hours
Name of Globe (White only) . . .	Dietz"Vulcan"No.39
*Regular Burner	No. 2 "Winglock" Rat.
Quantity Packed in Cases for Jobbing Trade	One Dozen

*For Kerosene, Substitute No. 1 "Winglock" Convex Burner.

PRICES, WEIGHTS AND MEASUREMENTS ARE GIVEN IN A SEPARATE PRICE LIST

R. E. DIETZ COMPANY - - - - - **NEW YORK, U. S. A.**

REAR SIGNAL LANTERN

"STEEL CLAD" FRAME

REG. U. S. PAT. OFFICE—PATENTED

**DIETZ
REAR SIGNAL LANTERN**

NO. 1 EXTRA SPECIAL
RATCHET BURNER
1" WICK

"VULCAN"
GLOBE

FOR SIGNAL OIL

DOZ.

Rear Signal Lanterns (Steel Clad), Bright Tin .   .   .   .

R. E. DIETZ COMPANY   -   -   -   -   -   **NEW YORK, U. S. A.**

REAR SIGNAL LANTERN

"STEEL CLAD" FRAME

REG. U. S. PAT. OFFICE—PATENTED

DIETZ REAR SIGNAL Lantern ("Steel Clad") is in considerable use by long-distance trolley systems who find it just as effective and far cheaper than the more elaborate Tail and Marker Lamps.

A standard bracket is provided, fitting the standard railroad socket. By using different colored globes the rear Signal Lantern becomes an efficient Marker Lamp.

For ease in cleaning, filling and lighting, this Lantern is not excelled. It has all the patented features of the Dietz "Steel Clad" Railroad Lantern and takes the standard railroad Lantern (No. 39) globe.

SPECIFICATIONS

Height Over All	$10\frac{1}{4}$ Inches
Volume of Light by Test (White) . .	2 C. Power
Size of Wick	1 Inch
Oil Used	"Signal"
Fount Capacity—Hours	24 Hours
Name of Globe	Dietz "Vulcan" (No. 39)
Regular Burner	No. 1 Extra Spec. Rat.
Quantity Packed in One Case . . .	One Dozen

PRICES, WEIGHTS AND MEASUREMENTS ARE GIVEN IN A SEPARATE PRICE LIST

R. E. DIETZ COMPANY - - - - - **NEW YORK, U. S. A.**

"VESTA" R. R. LANTERN
REG. U. S. PAT. OFFICE—PATENTED
(COLD BLAST)
A MODERN MONEY SAVER

The United States Army, many Elevated Railways, Subways and River Tunnels, Marine Departments of Coastal Railroads and other important users of traffic Lanterns use the Dietz "Vesta."

The "Vesta" is unexcelled for Police use in regulating street traffic.

R. E. DIETZ COMPANY   -   -   -   -   -   NEW YORK, U. S. A.

"VESTA" R. R. LANTERN

REG. U. S. PAT. OFFICE—PATENTED

(COLD BLAST)
A MODERN MONEY SAVER

TABLE SHOWING

THE ECONOMY OF USING

DIETZ "VESTA" LANTERN (KEROSENE) COMPARED WITH NO. 39 RAILROAD

LANTERNS (SIGNAL OIL)

PERFORMANCE	"VESTA" 150° KEROSENE	39 R. R. LANTERNS SIGNAL OIL
1 Gallon Oil Burns	224 Hours	347 Hours
Cost Per Gallon	10c. (Average)	37½c. (Average)
In 30 12-hour Days, Burns . .	52 Gills	34 Gills
Cost of Oil Burned	16c. Per Month	40c. per Month
Candle Power	3 C. Power	1 C. Power

1 "Vesta" Saves	-	-	24c. per Month in Oil
100 "Vestas" Save	-	$24.00	" " " "
1000 "Vestas" Save	-	$240.00	" " " "

IS THIS NOT WORTH WHILE?

DIETZ "VESTA"—A KEROSENE LANTERN FOR RAILROADS

Do you know that many Railroads use practically the same type of Signal Oil Lanterns in vogue 50 years ago? The modern Dietz "Vesta" R. R. Lantern burns kerosene at one-third the cost, gives three times the light; makes all railroad signals without blowing out.

R. E. DIETZ COMPANY - - - - - **NEW YORK, U. S. A.**

"VESTA" R. R. LANTERN

REG. U. S. PAT. OFFICE—PATENTED

(COLD BLAST)

**DIETZ
"VESTA"
RAILROAD LANTERN
BRIGHT TIN**

**DIETZ
"VESTA"
RAILROAD LANTERN
BRASS**

NO. 500 BURNER
3/8" WICK

"VESTA"
GLOBE

FOR KEROSENE

	DOZ.
Vesta R.R. Lanterns, Bright Tin	
Vesta R.R. Lanterns, Brass	

R. E. DIETZ COMPANY - - - - - **NEW YORK, U. S A.**

"VESTA" R. R. LANTERN

REG. U. S. PAT. OFFICE—PATENTED

(COLD BLAST)

DIETZ "VESTA" Railroad Lantern is of the modern Cold Blast construction, burns Kerosene and performs all the functions of the old-time Signal Oil Lantern in a superior way.

Like all types of Railroad Lanterns, the globe is removed through the frame by turning back the hinged top. The fount locks to the body of the Lantern by a patented positive-locking device operated by a twist of the hand. The flame is regulated from outside of the globe.

The "Vesta" fills every demand for an ideal Railroad Hand Lantern. It is easily cleaned, filled and lighted, is economical and positively makes all signals.

SPECIFICATIONS

Height Over All	11 Inches
Volume of Light by Test	3 C. Power
Size of Wick	⅜ Inch
Oil Used	150° Kerosene
Fount Capacity—Hours	16 Hours
Name of Globe (White, Ruby, Blue or Green) . .	Dietz "Vesta"
Patented Burner	No. 500
Quantity Packed in One Case	One Dozen

PRICES, WEIGHTS AND MEASUREMENTS ARE GIVEN IN A SEPARATE PRICE LIST

R. E. DIETZ COMPANY - - - - - - **NEW YORK, U. S. A.**

"IDEAL" INSPECTOR'S LANTERN

REG. U. S. PAT. OFFICE—PATENTED

(COLD BLAST)

**DIETZ
"IDEAL" INSPECTOR'S
LANTERN**

NO. 211 WING-LOCK BURNER
RISING CONE, 5/8" WICK

4" SILVERED REFLECTOR

"VESTA"
HEAT RESISTING
GLOBE

FOR KEROSENE

DOZ.

Ideal Inspector's Lanterns, Black Enamel . . . .

R. E. DIETZ COMPANY - - - - - **NEW YORK, U. S. A.**

"IDEAL" INSPECTOR'S LANTERN

REG. U. S. PAT. OFFICE—PATENTED

(COLD BLAST)

DIETZ "IDEAL" Inspector's Lantern is small and compact, being but 11½ inches high. It gives a reflected light of 15 candle power.

The "Ideal" is equipped with a bail for carrying on the arm and a patented non-heating grip handle. It has a large oil fount and the wick is exposed for trimming and lighting by lifting up the globe.

Car Inspectors, Ticket Collectors, Car Checkers and others find the "Ideal" very handy for their work. Nicely finished in Black Enamel.

The "Ideal" is furnished at a small extra charge, with a wire guard protecting the globe.

SPECIFICATIONS

Height Over All	11½ Inches
Reflected Light by Test	15 C. Power
Size of Wick	⅝ Inch
Oil Used	150° Kerosene
Fount Capacity—Hours	18 Hours
Name of Heat Resisting Globe	Dietz "Vesta"
Patented Tinned Steel Burner (Rising Cone)	No. 211
Reflector	4 Inches
Quantity Packed in One Case	Half Dozen

PRICES, WEIGHTS AND MEASUREMENTS ARE GIVEN IN A SEPARATE PRICE LIST

R. E. DIETZ COMPANY   -   -   -   -   -   NEW YORK, U. S. A.

"ACME" INSPECTOR'S LANTERN

REG. U. S. PAT. OFFICE—PATENTED

(HOT BLAST)

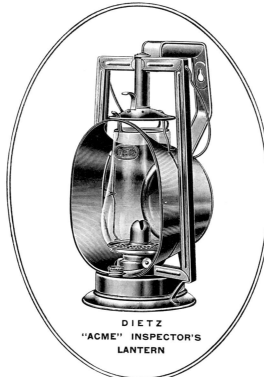

**DIETZ
"ACME" INSPECTOR'S
LANTERN**

NO. 551 WING-LOCK BURNER
LONG CONE, 5/8" WICK

6" SILVERED REFLECTOR

"FITZALL"
GLOBE

FOR KEROSENE

Acme Inspector's Lanterns, Bright Tin . . . . .

DOZ.

R. E. DIETZ COMPANY - - - - - NEW YORK, U. S. A.

"ACME" INSPECTOR'S LANTERN

REG. U. S. PAT. OFFICE—PATENTED

(HOT BLAST)

DIETZ "ACME" INSPECTOR'S Lantern is strongly made. Frame and hood are heavily braced and a strip of flat steel, well soldered, reinforces the frame.

The "Acme" gives a reflected light of 20 candle power. It is provided with a grip handle set at the right angle to project the light under cars, etc., and also has a hand bail.

Before the introduction of this Lantern, inspections were conducted with smoky oil torches. Most of the prominent railway systems have adopted the Dietz "Acme" as their standard Inspector's Lantern.

The "Acme" is furnished at a small extra charge, with a wire guard protecting the globe.

SPECIFICATIONS

Height Over All	15½ Inches
Reflected Light by Test	20 C. Power
Size of Wick	⅝ Inch
Oil Used	150° Kerosene
Fount Capacity—Hours	20 Hours
Name of Globe	Dietz "Fitzall"
Tinned Steel Winglock Burner (Long Cone)	No. 551
Silvered Glass Reflector	5 Inches
Quantity Packed in One Case	Half Dozen

PRICES, WEIGHTS AND MEASUREMENTS ARE GIVEN IN A SEPARATE PRICE LIST

R. E. DIETZ COMPANY - - - - - - NEW YORK, U. S. A.

"PROTECTOR" TRACKWALKER'S LANTERN

REG. U. S. PAT. OFFICE—PATENTED

(HOT BLAST)

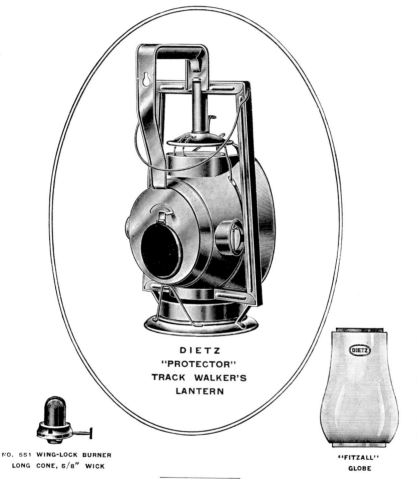

DIETZ
"PROTECTOR"
TRACK WALKER'S
LANTERN

NO. 551 WING-LOCK BURNER
LONG CONE, 5/8″ WICK

"FITZALL"
GLOBE

FOR KEROSENE

DOZ.

Protector Trackwalkers' Lanterns, Bright Tin . . . .

"PROTECTOR" TRACKWALKER'S LANTERN

REG. U. S. PAT. OFFICE—PATENTED

(HOT BLAST)

DIETZ "PROTECTOR." Trackwalker's Lantern is indispensable to the railroad night trackwalker.

The strong reflected light quickly detects the impairments of rails, joints, bolts and spikes which might lead to a wreck. A white 3-inch fixed semaphore lens in the back of the hood protects the trackwalker from being run down, and a ruby disc may be thrown between the white lens and the flame, instantly transforming the Lantern into a danger signal.

The Pennsylvania have, and other large systems are adopting the "Protector" Lantern in place of the dangerous makeshift lights formerly carried by the trackwalkers.

SPECIFICATIONS

Height Over All	15½ Inches
Reflected Light by Test	10 C. Power
Size of Wick	⅝ Inch
Oil Used	150° Kerosene
Fount Capacity—Hours	20 Hours
Name of Globe	Dietz "Fitzall"
Tinned Steel Burner (Long Cone)	No. 551
Quantity Packed in One Case	Half Dozen

PRICES, WEIGHTS AND MEASUREMENTS ARE GIVEN IN SEPARATE PRICE LIST

R. E. DIETZ COMPANY - - - - - **NEW YORK, U. S. A.**

TINNED STEEL BURNERS

PATENTED

FOR KEROSENE

NO. 101 BURNER
5/8 INCH WICK

NOS. 111 AND 162 BURNERS
5/8 AND 1 INCH WICKS

NO. 201 WING-LOCK BURNER
WING-LOCK CONE
5/8 INCH WICK

NO. 211 "RISING CONE"
WING-LOCK BURNER
5/8 INCH WICK

NO. 221 BURNER
SLOTTED CONE
5/8 INCH WICK

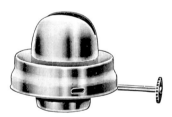

NO. 252 BURNER
SLOTTED CONE
1 INCH WICK

NO. 262 WING-LOCK BURNER
WING-LOCK CONE
1 INCH WICK

NO. 272 WING-LOCK BURNER
RISING CONE
1 INCH WICK

R. E. DIETZ COMPANY - - - - - **NEW YORK, U. S. A.**

TINNED STEEL BURNERS

PATENTED

FOR KEROSENE

THE BURNER makes a success or a failure of a Lantern. The marked superiority of Dietz Lanterns to all others is largely due to the Dietz patented Tinned Steel Burners.

NO. 101 Burner (chimney), ⅝-inch wick, for Bestov Lamps.

NO. 111 Burner (chimney), ⅝-inch wick, for No. 1 Climax Lanterns.

NO. 162 Burner (chimney), 1-inch wick, for No. 2 Climax Lanterns.

NO. 201 Burner, winglock cone, ⅝-inch wick, for Junior Lanterns and Junior Wagon Lanterns.

NO. 211 Burner, rising cone, ⅝-inch wick, for Little Wizard Lanterns, Roadster Wagon Lanterns and Ideal Inspectors' Lanterns.

NO. 221 Burner, slotted cone, ⅝-inch wick, for No. 15 Wall Lanterns.

NO. 252 Burner, slotted cone, 1-inch wick, for No. 2 Blizzard Mill Lanterns.

NO. 262 Burner, winglock cone, 1-inch wick, for No. 2 Crescent Lanterns, No. 25 Wall Lanterns and No. 30 Beacon Wall Lanterns.

NO. 272 Burner, rising cone, 1-inch wick, for No. 2 Blizzard Lanterns, No. 2 Large Fount Blizzard Lanterns, No. 2 Blizzard Dash Lanterns, No. 2 Wizard Lanterns, No. 2 Wizard Wagon Lanterns, No. 2 Wizard Fire Dep't Lanterns and No. 2 Wizard Inspectors' Lanterns.

PRICES, WEIGHTS AND MEASUREMENTS ARE GIVEN IN A SEPARATE PRICE LIST

R. E. DIETZ COMPANY - - - - - **NEW YORK, U. S. A.**

TINNED STEEL BURNERS

PATENTED

FOR KEROSENE

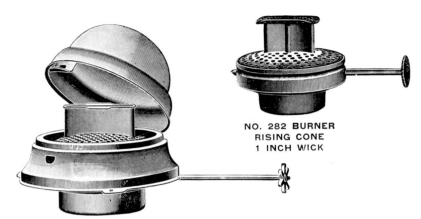

NO. 282 BURNER
RISING CONE
1 INCH WICK

NO. 303-313-323 BURNERS
WING-LOCK CONE
1 1/2 INCH WICK

NO. 351 BURNER
(NO. 1 CONVEX)
5/8 INCH WICK

NO. 371 BURNER
(SPEC. NO. 1 CONVEX)
5/8 INCH WICK

NO. 401 BURNER
PLAIN CONE
5/8 INCH WICK

NO. 411 BURNER
WING-LOCK CONE
5/8 INCH WICK

R. E. DIETZ COMPANY - - - - - NEW YORK, U. S. A.

TINNED STEEL BURNERS

PATENTED

FOR KEROSENE

DIETZ TINNED STEEL Burners are far superior to the brass burners of bygone days. They do not break down, are cooler, give a whiter flame and last during the life of the Lantern.

NO. 282 Burner, rising cone, 1-inch wick, for D-lite Lanterns.

NO. 303 Burner, winglock cone, 1½-inch wick, with long shaft (cog) for Imperial Platform Lanterns.

NO. 313 Burner, winglock cone, 1½-inch wick, with long shaft (button) for Pioneer Street and Hanging Lanterns.

NO. 323 Burner, winglock cone, 1½-inch wick, with short shaft (button), for No. 60 Beacon Wall Lanterns.

NO. 351 Burner (No. 1 Convex), ⅝-inch wick, for A No. 1 Lanterns and No. 6 Railroad Lanterns.

NO. 371 Burner (special No. 1 Convex), ⅝-inch wick, for U. S. Lanterns.

NO. 401 Burner, plain cone, ⅝-inch wick, for O. K. Lanterns. Substitute for regular burner on Monarch, Crystal and Iron Clad Lanterns, Underwriter's Mill Lanterns and King Fire Dep't Lanterns.

NO. 411 Burner, winglock cone, ⅝-inch wick, for Little Star, Victor and Monarch Lanterns, Buckeye Dash Lanterns and Victor Wagon Lanterns.

PRICES, WEIGHTS AND MEASUREMENTS ARE GIVEN IN A SEPARATE PRICE LIST

R. E. DIETZ COMPANY   -   -   -   -   NEW YORK, U. S. A.

TINNED STEEL BURNERS

PATENTED

FOR KEROSENE

NO. 421 BURNER
HINGED CONE
5/8 INCH WICK

NO. 462 BURNER
WING-LOCK CONE
1 INCH WICK

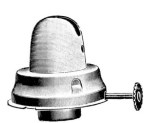

NO. 500 BURNER
3/8 INCH WICK

NO. 510 BURNER
3/8 INCH WICK

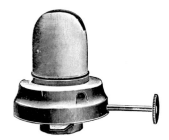

NO. 551 WING-LOCK BURNER
5/8 INCH WICK

NO. 561 WING-LOCK BURNER
5/8 INCH WICK

R. E. DIETZ COMPANY   -   -   -   -   -   NEW YORK, U. S. A.

TINNED STEEL BURNERS

PATENTED

FOR KEROSENE

BALANCED AIR CIRCULATION in Dietz Tubular Lanterns is made 100 per cent effective in light-giving by the use of Dietz patented Tinned Steel Burners.

NO. 421 Burner, hinged cone, ⅝-inch wick, for Hy-lo, Crystal and Iron Clad Lanterns, Underwriter's Mill and King Fire Dep't Lanterns.

NO. 462 Burner, winglock cone, 1-inch wick, for No. 2 Royal Lanterns.

NO. 500 Burner, long cone, ⅜-inch wick, for Vesta Lanterns.

NO. 510 Burner,'long cone, ⅜-inch wick, for Octo and Union Driving Lanterns.

NO. 551 Burner, long cone, ⅝-inch wick, for Beacon Dash Lanterns, Acme Inspector Lanterns and Protector Trackwalker's Lanterns.

NO. 561 Wing-lock Burner, ⅝-inch wick, for Eureka Driving Lanterns.

PRICES, WEIGHTS AND MEASUREMENTS ARE GIVEN IN A SEPARATE PRICE LIST

R. E. DIETZ COMPANY - - - - - **NEW YORK, U. S. A.**

R. R. LANTERN BURNERS

PATENTED

KEROSENE AND SIGNAL OIL

NO. 601 SPECIAL RATCHET
BURNER
SIGNAL OIL—5/8 INCH WICK

NO. 652 WICK SCRAPER
RATCHET BURNER
SIGNAL OIL—1 INCH WICK

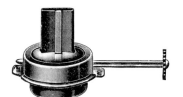

NO. 1 WING-LOCK
RATCHET BURNER
SIGNAL OIL—5/8 INCH WICK

NO. 2 WING-LOCK
RATCHET BURNER
SIGNAL OIL—1 INCH WICK

NO. 1 WING-LOCK
CONVEX BURNER
KEROSENE—5/8 INCH WICK

NO. 1
RATCHET BURNER
SIGNAL OIL—5/8 INCH WICK

NO. 1 EXTRA SPECIAL
RATCHET BURNER
SIGNAL OIL—1 INCH WICK

NO. 2
RATCHET BURNER
SIGNAL OIL—1 INCH WICK

R. E. DIETZ COMPANY   -   -   -   -   -   NEW YORK, U. S. A.

R. R. LANTERN BURNERS
PATENTED
KEROSENE AND SIGNAL OIL

NO. 601 Special ratchet Burner, (signal oil), ⅝-inch wick, for Police Lanterns.

NO. 652 Wickscraper ratchet Burner (signal oil), 1-inch wick, for Watchman's Mill Lantern.

NO. 1 WINGLOCK ratchet Burner (signal oil), ⅝-inch wick, slip collar, for Dietz Standard, Vulcan and Steel Clad Railroad Lanterns.

NO. 2 WINGLOCK ratchet Burner (signal oil), 1-inch wick, slip collar, for Dietz Standard, Vulcan and Steel Clad Railroad Lanterns.

NO. 1 WINGLOCK Convex Burner (kerosene), ⅝-inch wick, slip collar, for Dietz Standard, Vulcan and Steel Clad Railroad Lanterns.

NO. 1 SCREW COLLAR ratchet Burner (signal oil), ⅝-inch wick, for Dietz No. 6 Railroad Lanterns.

NO. 1 EXTRA SPECIAL SCREW COLLAR ratchet Burner (signal oil), 1-inch wick, for Dietz Rear Signal Lanterns.

NO. 2 SCREW COLLAR ratchet Burner (signal oil), 1-inch wick, for Dietz No. 6 Railroad Lanterns.

PRICES, WEIGHTS AND MEASUREMENTS ARE GIVEN IN A SEPARATE PRICE LIST

R. E. DIETZ COMPANY - - - - - **NEW YORK, U. S. A.**

DRIVING LANTERN HOLDERS

FOR WAGONS AND CARRIAGES

BLACK ENAMEL FINISH

"A"
STEEL DASH CLAMP
HOLDER

"B"
STEEL FINGER PROP
HOLDER

"E"
FLAT BRACKET
HOLDER

"R"
BUGGY TOP (RAIL)
HOLDER

"W"
TUBULAR LANTERN
HOLDER

STREET LANTERN
BRACKET
20 INCHES LONG

R. E. DIETZ COMPANY   -   -   -   -   -   NEW YORK, U. S. A.

DRIVING LANTERN HOLDERS

FOR WAGONS AND CARRIAGES

BLACK ENAMEL FINISH

DIETZ LANTERN HOLDERS are adapted to all types of Wagons and Carriages. All Dietz Wagon Lanterns are equipped with a combination socket permitting the use of a round or flat bracket. By the use of Lantern Holders "A," "B," and "R," a Driving Lantern may be located on a vehicle's dash, the end of the seat, on the body or on the buggy top.

"A"—Dash Clamp Holder. For use with Victor, Junior Roadster and No. 2 Wizard Wagon Lanterns, also Eureka, Octo and Union Driving Lanterns.

"B"—Finger Prop Holder. For use with Victor, Junior, Roadster and No. 2 Wizard Wagon Lanterns, also Eureka, Octo and Union Driving Lanterns.

"E"—Flat Bracket Holder. For use with Victor, Junior, Roadster and No. 2 Wizard Wagon Lanterns.

"R"—Buggy Top (rail) Holder. For use with Victor, Junior, Roadster and No. 2 Wizard Wagon Lanterns, also Eureka, Octo and Union Driving Lanterns.

STREET LANTERN BRACKET

Street Lantern Bracket. 20 inches long, for Pioneer Street Lanterns.

PRICES, WEIGHTS AND MEASUREMENTS ARE GIVEN IN A SEPARATE PRICE LIST

R. E. DIETZ COMPANY - - - - - **NEW YORK, U. S. A.**

SELECTED LANTERN GLOBES

FROM EXCLUSIVE DIETZ MOULDS

TRADE MARKED

Colors—White, Ruby, Blue and Green

"JUNIOR" GLOBE
5 1/2 IN. HIGH
TOP 2 3/8 IN. WIDE
BOTTOM 2 13/16 IN.
WIDE

"LITTLE STAR U. S."
5 1/2 IN. HIGH
TOP 2 7/16 IN. WIDE
BOTTOM 2 13/16 IN.
WIDE

"FITZALL" GLOBE
6 9/16 IN. HIGH
TOP 2 13/16 IN. WIDE
BOTTOM 3 7/16 IN. WIDE

"BLIZZARD" GLOBE
6 5/8 IN. HIGH
TOP 2 13/16 IN. WIDE
BOTTOM 3 7/16 IN. WIDE

"BLIZZARD" LOC-NOB GLOBE
6 5/8 IN. HIGH
TOP 2 13/16 IN. WIDE
BOTTOM 3 7/16 IN. WIDE

"LITTLE WIZARD"
GLOBE
3 13/16 IN. HIGH
TOP 3 1/4 IN. WIDE
BOTTOM 2 13/16 IN.
WIDE

"LITTLE WIZARD"
LOC-NOB GLOBE
3 13/16 IN. HIGH
TOP 3 1/4 IN. WIDE
BOTTOM 2 13/16 IN.
WIDE

"D-LITE" GLOBE
4 9/16 IN. HIGH
TOP 4 IN. WIDE
BOTTOM 3 7/16 IN.
WIDE

"D-LITE" LOC-NOB GLOBE
4 9/16 IN. HIGH
TOP 4 IN. WIDE
BOTTOM 3 7/16 IN.
WIDE

"NO. 2 TUBULAR" GLOBE
9 IN. HIGH
TOP 4 5/16 IN. WIDE
BOTTOM 5 IN.
WIDE

"PIONEER" GLOBE
10 3/4 IN. HIGH
TOP 5 3/4 IN. WIDE
BOTTOM 6 IN. WIDE

R. E. DIETZ COMPANY - - - - - **NEW YORK, U. S. A.**

SELECTED LANTERN GLOBES

FROM EXCLUSIVE DIETZ MOULDS

TRADE MARKED

Colors—White, Ruby, Blue and Green.

JUNIOR Globes: For Junior Lanterns and Junior Wagon Lanterns.

LITTLE STAR-U. S. Globes: For Little Star and U. S. Lanterns.

FITZALL Globes: For Hy-lo, Victor, Monarch, O. K., Crystal, Iron Clad, Royal and Crescent Lanterns, Buckeye and Beacon Dash Lanterns, Victor Wagon Lanterns, King Fire Dep't Lanterns, Underwriter's Mill Lanterns, No. 15 Wall Lanterns, A No. 1 Lanterns, Acme Inspector's Lanterns and Protector Trackwalker's Lanterns.

BLIZZARD Globes (Without Loc-Nobs): For No. 2 Blizzard Dash Lanterns, No. 2 Blizzard Mill Lanterns and No. 30 Beacon Wall Lanterns.

BLIZZARD–LOC-NOB Globes: For No. 2 Blizzard and Special No. 2 Blizzard Lanterns.

LITTLE WIZARD Globes (Without Loc-Nobs): For Roadster Wagon Lanterns

LITTLE WIZARD–LOC-NOB Globes· For Little Wizard Lanterns.

D-LITE Globes (Without Loc-Nobs): For No. 2 Wizard Wagon Lanterns, No. 2 Wizard Fire Dep't Lanterns and No. 2 Wizard Inspector's Lanterns.

D-LITE–LOC-NOB Globes: For Wizard and D-lite Lanterns.

NO. 2 TUBULAR Globes: For No. 60 Beacon Wall Lanterns.

PIONEER Globes: For Pioneer Street and Hanging Lanterns.

PRICES, WEIGHTS AND MEASUREMENTS ARE GIVEN IN A SEPARATE PRICE LIST

R. E. DIETZ COMPANY - · - · - **NEW YORK, U. S. A.**

RAILROAD LANTERN GLOBES

FROM EXCLUSIVE DIETZ MOULDS

TRADE MARKED

Colors—White, Ruby, Blue and Green

"VESTA" GLOBE
4 1/4 IN. HIGH
TOP 2 5/16 WIDE
BOTTOM 2 13/16 IN. WIDE

"VULCAN" (NO. 39) GLOBE
4 7/8 IN. HIGH
TOP 2 13/16 IN. WIDE
BOTTOM 3 3/8 IN. WIDE

SILVERED GLASS
REFLECTORS
4 IN., 5 IN., 7 IN., 8 IN.

"NO. 6 R. R." GLOBE
5 7/8 IN. HIGH
TOP 2 5/8 IN. WIDE
BOTTOM 3 9/16 IN. WIDE

R. E. DIETZ COMPANY - - - - - **NEW YORK, U. S. A.**

RAILROAD LANTERN GLOBES

FROM EXCLUSIVE DIETZ MOULDS

TRADE MARKED

Colors—White, Ruby, Blue and Green.

VESTA Globes: For Vesta Railroad Lanterns and Ideal Inspector's Lanterns.

VULCAN (NO. 39) Globes: For Standard, Vulcan and Steel Clad Railroad Lanterns, X. L. C. R. Switchmen's Lanterns, Watchman's Lanterns and Rear Signal Lanterns.

NO. 6 RAILROAD Globes: For No. 6 Railroad Lanterns.

SILVERED GLASS REFLECTORS

4-Inch (flat back) silvered glass reflectors: For Ideal Inspectors' Lanterns.

5-Inch (flat back) silvered glass reflectors: For Beacon Dash Lanterns, No. 60 Beacon Wall Lanterns and Acme Inspector's Lanterns.

5-Inch (regular) silvered glass reflectors: For No. 15 Wall Lanterns.

7-Inch (regular) silvered glass reflectors: For No. 1 Climax Platform Lanterns.

8-Inch (regular) silvered glass reflectors: For Imperial and No. 2 Climax Platform Lanterns.

PRICES, WEIGHTS AND MEASUREMENTS ARE GIVEN IN A SEPARATE PRICE LIST

R. E. DIETZ COMPANY - - - - - **NEW YORK, U. S. A.**

FOREIGN SALES AGENTS

STRONG & TROWBRIDGE CO.
LONDON, ENGLAND

ELLIOTT & CO.
CALCUTTA, INDIA

W. H. BRADY & CO., Ltd.
BOMBAY, INDIA

R. W. WINNING
SYDNEY, N. S. W., AUSTRALIA

CHARLES A. POPE
{ BUENOS AIRES, ARGENTINA
{ VALPARAISO, CHILE

CHARLES V. HITCHINS
MEXICO CITY, MEXICO

J. A. VAZQUEZ
HAVANA, CUBA

E. F. RODRIGUEZ
SAN JUAN, PORTO RICO

A. & BENJ. GOMES CASSERES
BARRANQUILLA, COLOMBIA

LAWRENCE NEWFOUNDLAND CO., Ltd.
ST. JOHNS, NEWFOUNDLAND

E. & A. YOULDON
JOHANNESBURG, SOUTH AFRICA

H. KETTLES ROY
NAIROBI, BRITISH EAST AFRICA

G. LARREATEGUI
GUAYAQUIL, ECUADOR

JOHN WILSON
PORT-OF-SPAIN, TRINIDAD, B. W. I.

JOSE SAN MARTIN
CARACAS, VENEZUELA

R. E. DIETZ COMPANY - - - - - NEW YORK, U. S. A.

EXPORT METHODS

WE CONDUCT CORRESPONDENCE in the language desired by our foreign customers.

OUR METHOD OF PACKING Lanterns minimizes weight and cubic contents, and the goods carry safely to any part of the world.

SHIPPING DIRECTIONS, marks and numbering, delivery and insurance instructions, etc., are faithfully followed in accordance with customers' specifications.

INVOICES, BILLS OF LADING, Consular documents, etc., *are executed in exact accordance with the laws of the various countries to which our Lanterns are shipped,* thereby protecting our customers against *fines* and *penalties.*

DELIVERIES ALONGSIDE STEAMER are facilitated through direct rail connections from our factory railroad sidings to the wharves.

NEW INDENTORS will facilitate shipments by establishing banking credit in New York City or forwarding United States references with first order.

R. E. DIETZ COMPANY   -   -   -   -   -   NEW YORK, U. S. A.

OLD-TIME LANTERN FACTORY
NEW YORK CITY

EARLY DIETZ LANTERN FACTORY

FULTON AND CLIFF STS., N. Y. (12,000 SQUARE FEET)

IN THE EARLY DAYS of the *Tubular* Lantern industry, DIETZ Lanterns were all made on the three upper floors of the building illustrated above. Here, too, appeared the first "Cold Blast" Street Lantern, and the DIETZ "UNION" Driving Lantern, the progenitor of all "Cold Blast" Motor Car Lights.

THE GROWTH OF THE INDUSTRY was steady, and with the passing of the years the Fulton Street plant became cramped and ground at Greenwich and Laight Streets was bought and a modern factory of fireproof construction was erected by R. E. DIETZ.

R. E. DIETZ COMPANY - - - - - **NEW YORK, U. S. A.**

MODERN LANTERN FACTORIES
NEW YORK AND SYRACUSE

AT SYRACUSE, NEW YORK—OVER 164,246 SQUARE FEET

THE DIETZ LANTERN FACTORIES OF TO-DAY—LARGEST IN THE WORLD

AT NEW YORK CITY—OVER 97,202 SQUARE FEET

THE expansion of the Tubular Lantern business from three floors to the present acreage is strikingly shown in the perspective view of our New York City and Syracuse buildings, combined in the above illustration.

THE DIETZ LANTERN FACTORY at Syracuse, N.Y., is located on Wilkinson Street, opposite Leavenworth Park, about 5 minutes' walk from the New York Central Station. Main buildings are of mill construction. Every modern device is employed to safeguard the employees and facilitate production.

THE DIETZ LANTERN FACTORY in New York City is located in the nine-story and basement fire-proof Dietz Building, Greenwich at Laight Street, a short distance from Desbrosses Street Ferry. Here are made not only Lanterns but Motor Truck Lamps and the tinned steel burners used in Dietz Lanterns.

THE GENERAL OFFICES OF THE COMPANY ARE IN THE NEW YORK CITY BUILDING, No. SIXTY LAIGHT ST.

R. E. DIETZ COMPANY   -   -   -   -   NEW YORK, U. S. A.

TUBULAR LANTERN TYPES

HOT BLAST—COLD BLAST

DEFINED

TYPE OF
"HOT BLAST"
LANTERN
WITH BELL TOP

**DIETZ
"LITTLE STAR"**
(HOT BLAST)

NEW TYPE OF
"COLD BLAST"
LANTERN
WITH CHIMNEY TOP

**DIETZ
"LITTLE WIZARD"**
(COLD BLAST)
WITH SHORT GLOBE

R. E. DIETZ COMPANY -   -   -   -   -   **NEW YORK, U. S. A.**

TUBULAR LANTERN TYPES

HOT BLAST—COLD BLAST

DEFINED

TUBULAR LANTERNS are roughly classified under the captions "Hot Blast" and "Cold Blast." DIETZ made the first "Hot Blast" Lanterns in 1868, and the first "Cold Blast" Lanterns in 1880. On the opposite page a typical Lantern of each class is illustrated.

THE TERMS "HOT BLAST" AND "COLD BLAST" are used solely in connection with TUBULAR Lanterns and with regard to the method of supplying air to the flame.

A "HOT BLAST" Tubular Lantern is so constructed that a supply of fresh air enters the globe at the base through the openings in the perforated globe plate. This fresh air, in ascending through the globe, becomes heated by the flame and mingles with the hot products of combustion. A portion of this mixture of hot air and spent gases passes into the bell or canopy over the globe and through the side tubes to the air chamber beneath the burner, there directly supplying the flame.

A "COLD BLAST" Tubular Lantern is so constructed that the supply of air taken through the side tubes does not mingle with the products of combustion and the flame is supplied with fresh air both through the globe plate and the side tubes. A white light is thus secured where the flame of a "Hot Blast" Lantern has a yellowish tinge. The spent products of combustion escape to the outer air through a central metal chimney in the Lantern head. From an air chamber surrounding the metal chimney, which is provided with injectors for taking in air, fresh air is taken into the side tubes, down which it flows to the lower air chamber and thus to the burner. THE FACT THAT THE "COLD BLAST" LANTERN PRODUCES A PERFECTLY WHITE FLAME AND A SUPERIOR VOLUME OF LIGHT HAS RENDERED THIS TYPE OF TUBULAR LANTERN A FAVORITE WITH USERS.

R. E. DIETZ COMPANY - - - - - NEW YORK, U S. A.

QUALITY LANTERN TAGS

INSIST ON THE LANTERN WITH THE YELLOW TAG

DIETZ

QUALITY TAG
Is attached to each GENUINE DIETZ LANTERN as a guarantee of QUALITY and PERFECTION. All DIETZ LANTERNS are carefully inspected. You take no risk when buying a DIETZ make as the DIETZ reputation stands back of each LANTERN. DIETZ makes a LANTERN for Every Purpose; be sure this is the right one for your use.

R. E. DIETZ COMPANY
Largest Makers of Lanterns in the World
Established 1840
New York, U. S. A.
(over)

SINCE DIETZ introduced the Original Tubular Lantern over 45 years ago, cheap, inferior imitations have appeared from year to year, yet absolute merit has enabled us to attain during that time the proud distinction of being *"The Largest Makers of Lanterns in the World."*

All Genuine Dietz Lanterns Are Plainly Stamped REGISTERED **DIETZ** U. S. PAT. OFF.

THAT it may not be forgotten that "DIETZ" Lanterns are *"Different"* from the host of imitations (with merely the outward appearance of our line), we aim to have each Lantern of the DIETZ Standard Brand stamped REGISTERED **DIETZ** U. S. PAT. OFF. with the name— and tagged with a yellow "Quality" tag, bearing our trade-mark.

FOR VALUE

DIETZ

REG. U. S. PAT. OFF.

LANTERNS
Have always been the Best

Sold wherever the Sun Shines
Used wherever the Sun Sets

Keep this Lantern Clean

Price...................Each
(over)

R. E. DIETZ COMPANY　·　·　·　·　·　**NEW YORK, U. S. A.**

SUPERIOR LANTERN PACKAGES

TRAVEL BY RAIL, WATER OR BY MULE BACK—ARRIVE INTACT!

THE ABOVE IS AN ILLUSTRATION of a DIETZ standard package. It holds one dozen DIETZ "VICTOR" Lanterns snugly packed in heavy paper bags without excelsior, hay or other packing. We originated this method over thirty-seven years ago, minimizing weight and cubic contents, and it is the most satisfactory and clean way for domestic or foreign trade.

THE OUTSIDE DIMENSIONS of the above case are: thirty-one inches long, fifteen inches wide, and eleven inches deep, totaling three cubic feet and weighing gross, approximately thirty-five pounds.

DIETZ LANTERN CASES ARE MADE of white pine: sides, top and bottom are half-inch, ends seven-eighths stock. Ends are neatly printed showing the contents and the sides are marked

THESE CASES ARE SEEN in every port of the world and we are in receipt of many interesting photographs showing natives of India, Africa, etc., unloading them or carrying them in and out of the "Go-downs" or storehouses.

R. E. DIETZ COMPANY - - - - - NEW YORK, U. S. A.

NO. 12 LANTERN DISPLAY

A STAND WITH 12 STYLES OF LANTERNS

ATTRACTIVELY DISPLAYED

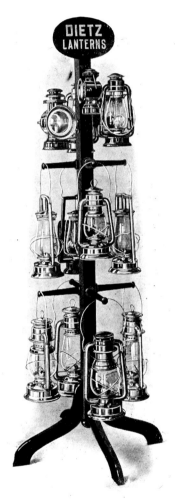

TOTAL HEIGHT	SPREAD AT BASE
70 INCHES	29 INCHES

EACH

No. 12 Lantern Display with 12 Lanterns .   .   .   .   .   .

R. E. DIETZ COMPANY - - - - - **NEW YORK, U. S. A.**

NO. 12 LANTERN DISPLAY

A STAND WITH 12 STYLES OF LANTERNS
ATTRACTIVELY DISPLAYED

The DIETZ No. 12 Lantern Display Stand is designed to do effective work as a "Silent Salesman."

No Domestic Jobber or Retailer, and no Foreign Indentor or Dealer, handling Lanterns, can afford to be without this business-bringer.

Remember: "Goods well displayed are half sold." And a man buying one Lantern from a DIETZ Display Stand is liable to buy other styles also.

A DIETZ Display Stand in a show window will sell Lanterns from the street.   To see a fine DIETZ Lantern creates a desire to own it.

The Display Stand is made of fumed oak and is attractive in itself.   The displays are not sold direct to the retailer but through Jobbers and the Export Trade.   They carry a good profit.

PRICES, WEIGHTS AND MEASUREMENTS ARE GIVEN IN A SEPARATE PRICE LIST

R. E. DIETZ COMPANY - - - - - **NEW YORK, U. S. A.**

COLD ROLLED STEEL MOTOR TRUCK LAMPS

(COLD BLAST)

**DIETZ
"ROYAL JUNIOR"
MOTOR TRUCK SIDE LAMPS**
FOR ½, 1 AND 2 TON TRUCKS

**DIETZ
"CHAMPION"
MOTOR TRUCK SIDE LAMP**
FOR 2, 3 AND 5 TON TRUCKS

INSIDE BRASS FOUNT
(NON-LOSEABLE)

FOR KEROSENE

WITHSTAND VIBRATION. WILL NOT JAR OR BLOW OUT.

R. E. DIETZ COMPANY - - - - NEW YORK, U. S. A.

COLD ROLLED STEEL MOTOR TRUCK LAMPS

(HOT BLAST)

DIETZ
"No. 2 IRON CLAD"
MOTOR TRUCK SIDE LAMP

MADE OF COLD ROLLED STEEL
FITTED WITH INSIDE BRASS
NON-LOSEABLE OIL FOUNTS
BEST QUALITY SIGNAL LENSES
GUARANTEED TO STAY LIGHTED
PRICES REASONABLE.

DIETZ
"No. 2 IRON CLAD"
MOTOR TRUCK TAIL LAMP

FOR KEROSENE

WRITE FOR COMPLETE CATALOGUE SHOWING ALL MODELS.

R. E. DIETZ COMPANY　-　-　-　-　-　-　NEW YORK, U. S. A.

Dietz Lantern Price Guide

The values in this book should be used only as a guide. These prices will vary from one section of the country to the other. All prices are also affected by the condition as well as the demand of the piece. Neither the Author nor the Publisher assumes responsibility for any losses or gains that might be incurred as a result of using this guide.

Page 2: **$400+**

Page 6: **$150+**

Page 8: **$20+**

Page 10: **$150+**

Page 12: **$60+**

Page 14: **$125+**

Page 16: **$175+**

Page 18: **$125+**

Page 20: **$30+**

Page 22: **$150+**

Page 24: **$750+**
(complete unit)

Page 25: **$500+**
(complete unit)

Page 26: **$65+**

Page 28: **$15+**

Page 30: **$50+**

Page 32: **$25+**

Page 34: **$15+**

Page 36: **$25+**

Page 38: **$50+**

Page 40: **$100+**

Page 42: **$50+**

Page 44: **$150+**

Page 46: **$60+**

Page 48: **$125+**

Page 50: **$35+**

Page 52: **$75+**

Page 54: **$75+**

Page 56: **$50+**

Page 58: **$50+**

Page 60: **$200+**

Page 62: **$150+**

Page 64: **$170+**

Page 66: **$150+**

Page 68: **$150+**

Page 70: **$40**
(Brass) **$60**

Page 72: **$100+**

Page 74: No. 30 - **$50+**
No. 60 - **$100+**

Page 76: **$75+**

Page 78: **$50+**

Page 80: **$300+**

Page 82: **$100+**

Page 84: **$100+**

Page 86: **$100+**

Page 88: **$175+**

Page 90: **$200+**

Page 92: **$40+**

Page 94: **$25+**

Page 96: **$25+**

Page 98: **$35+**

Page 100: **$225+**

Page 102: **$125+**

Page 104: **$35+**

Page 106: **$35+**
(Brass) **$100+**

Page 108: **$75+**

Page 110: **$100+**

Page 112: **$75+**

Page 132: **$125+**
"Little Wizard" **$15+**

Page 138: Both
on page **$200+**

Page 139: Both
on page **$250+**